DOVER · THRIFT · EDITIONS

The Recognition of Śakuntala

KALIDASA

Translated by Arthur W. Ryder
Introduction by Rabindranath Tagore

DOVER PUBLICATIONS, INC.
Mineola, New York

DOVER THRIFT EDITIONS

GENERAL EDITOR: PAUL NEGRI
EDITOR OF THIS VOLUME: SUSAN L. RATTINER

Copyright

Theatrical Rights

This Dover Thrift Edition may be used in its entirety, in adaptation, or in any other way for theatrical productions, professional and amateur, in the United States, without fee, permission, or acknowledgment. (This may not apply outside of the United States, as copyright conditions may vary.)

Bibliographical Note

This Dover edition, first published in 2003, is an unabridged republication of the Arthur W. Ryder translation of the seven-act play, as originally published by E. P. Dutton & Co., New York, in 1912 under the title *Kalidasa: Translations of Shakuntala and Other Works*. An introduction by Rabindranath Tagore, originally published in *Sakuntala* by Macmillan and Co., Ltd., London, in 1920, has been added to the present edition.

Library of Congress Cataloging-in-Publication Data

Kalidasa.
    [Sakuntala. English]
    The Recognition of Śakuntala / Kalidasa ; translated by Arthur W. Ryder ; introduction by Rabindranath Tagore.
       p. cm. — (Dover thrift editions)
    Originally published as: Kalidasa : translations of Shakuntala, and other works. New York : Dutton & Co., 1912.
    Translated from Sanskrit.
    ISBN 0-486-43169-X (pbk.)
    1. âákuntalâ (Hindu mythology)—Drama. I. Ryder, Arthur W. (Arthur William), 1877–1938. II. Title. III. Series.

PK3795.E5 2003
891'.22—dc21

2003048482

Manufactured in the United States of America
Dover Publications, Inc., 31 East 2nd Street, Mineola, N.Y. 11501

ŚAKUNTALA

ITS INNER MEANING

By RABINDRANATH TAGORE

Would'st thou the young year's blossoms
    and the fruits of its decline,
And all by which the soul is charmed,
    enraptured, feasted, fed,
Would'st thou the Earth and Heaven itself
    in one sole name combine?
I name thee, O Śakuntala! and all at
    once is said.

GOETHE.

GOETHE, the master-poet of Europe, has summed up his criticism of *Śakuntala* in a single quatrain; he has not taken the poem to pieces. This quatrain seems to be a small thing like the flame of a candle, but it lights up the whole drama in an instant, and reveals its inner nature. In Goethe's words, *Śakuntala* blends together the young year's blossoms and the fruits of maturity; it combines heaven and earth in one.

We are apt to pass over this eulogy lightly as a mere poetical outburst. We are apt to consider that it only means in effect that Goethe regarded *Śakuntala* as fine poetry. But it is not really so. His stanza breathes not the exaggeration of rapture, but the deliberate judgment of a true critic. There is a special point in his words. Goethe says expressly that *Śakuntala* contains the history of a development—the development of flower into fruit, of earth into heaven, of matter into spirit.

In truth there are two unions in *Śakuntala;* and the *motif* of the play is the progress from the earlier union of the first Act, with its earthly unstable beauty and romance, to the higher union in the heavenly hermitage of eternal bliss described in the last Act. This drama was meant not for dealing with a particular passion, not for developing a particular character, but for translating the whole subject from one world to another—to elevate love from the sphere of physical beauty to the eternal heaven of moral beauty.

With the greatest ease Kalidasa has effected this junction of earth with heaven. His earth so naturally passes into heaven that we do not mark the boundary-line between the two. In the First Act the poet has not concealed the gross earthiness of the fall of Śakuntala; he has clearly shown, in the conduct of the hero and heroine alike, how much desire contributed to that fall. He has fully painted all the blandishments, playfulness, and fluttering of the intoxicating sense of youth, the struggle between deep bashfulness and strong self-expression. This is a proof of the simplicity of Śakuntala; she was not prepared beforehand for the outburst of passion which the occasion of Dushyanta's visit called forth. Hence she had not learned how to restrain herself, how to hide her feelings. Śakuntala had not known Cupid before; hence her heart was bare of armour, and she could not distrust either the sentiment of love or the character of the lover. The daughter of the hermitage was off her guard, just as the deer there knew not fear.

Dushyanta's conquest of Śakuntala has been very naturally drawn. With equal ease has the poet shown the deeper purity of her character in spite of her fall—her unimpaired innate chastity. This is another proof of her simplicity.

The flower of the forest needs no servant to brush the dust off her petals. She stands bare; dust settles on her; but in spite of it she easily retains her own beautiful cleanliness. Dust did settle on Śakuntala, but she was not even conscious of it. Like the simple wild deer, like the mountain spring, she stood forth pure in spite of mud.

Kalidasa has let his hermitage-bred youthful heroine follow the unsuspecting path of Nature; nowhere has he restrained her. And yet he has developed her into the model of a devoted wife, with her reserve, endurance of sorrow, and life of rigid spiritual discipline. At the beginning, we see her self-forgetful and obedient to Nature's impulses like the plants and flowers; at the end we see her deeper feminine soul—sober, patient under ill, intent on austerities, strictly regulated by the sacred laws of piety. With matchless art Kalidasa has placed his heroine at the meeting-point of action and calmness, of Nature and Law, of river and ocean, as it were. Her father was a hermit, but her mother was a nymph. Her birth was the outcome of interrupted austerities, but her nurture was in a hermitage, which is just the spot where nature and austerities, beauty and restraint are harmonised. There is none of the conventional bonds of society there, yet we have the harder regulations of religion. Her *gandharva* marriage, too, was of the same type; it had the wildness of nature joined to the social tie of wedlock. The drama Śakuntala stands alone and unrivalled in all literature, because it depicts how Restraint can be harmonised with Freedom. All its joys and sorrows, unions and partings, proceed from the conflict of these two forces.

Śakuntala's simplicity is natural, that of Miranda is unnatural. The different circumstances under which the two were brought up account for this difference. Śakuntala's simplicity was not girt round with ignorance, as was the case with Miranda. We see in the First Act that Śakuntala's two companions did not let her remain unaware of the fact that she was in the first bloom of youth. She had learnt to be bashful. But all these things are external. Her simplicity, on the other hand, is more deeply seated, and so also is her purity. To the very end the poet shows that she had no experience of the outside world. Her simplicity is innate. True, she knew something of the world, because the hermitage did not stand altogether outside society; the rules of home life were observed here too. She was inexperienced though not ignorant of the outside world; but trustfulness was firmly enthroned in her heart. The simplicity which springs from such trustfulness had for a moment caused her fall, but it also redeemed her for ever. This trustfulness kept her constant to patience, forgiveness, and loving kindness, in spite of the cruellest breach of her confidence. Miranda's simplicity was never subjected to such a fiery ordeal; it never clashed with knowledge of the world.

Our rebellious passions raise storms. In this drama Kalidasa has extinguished the volcanic fire of tumultuous passion by means of the tears of the penitent heart. But he has not dwelt too long on the disease—he has just given a glimpse of it and then dropped the veil. The desertion of Śakuntala by the amorous Dushyanta, which in real life would have happened as the natural consequence of his character, is here brought about by the curse of Durvasa. Otherwise, the desertion would have been so extremely cruel and pathetic as to destroy the peace and harmony of the whole play. But the poet has left a small rent in the veil through which we can get an idea of the royal sin. It is in the Fifth Act. Just before Śakuntala arrives at court and is repudiated by her husband, the poet momentarily draws aside the curtain form the King's love affairs. A woman's voice is heard singing behind the scene:

O honey-bee! having sucked the mango-blossoms in your search for new honey, you have forgotten the recent loving welcome by the lotus!

This tear-stained song of a stricken heart in the royal household gives us a rude shock, especially as our heart was hitherto filled with Dushyanta's love-passages with Śakuntala. Only in the preceding Act we saw Śakuntala setting out for her husband's home in a very holy, sweet, and tender mood, carrying with herself the blessings of the hoary sage Kanwa and the good wishes of the whole forest world. And now a stain falls on the picture we had so hopefully formed of the home of love to which she was going.

When the jester asked, "What means this song?" Dushyanta smiled and said, "We desert our loves after a short spell of love-making, and therefore I have deserved this strong rebuke from Queen Hansa-padika." This indication of the fickleness of royal love is not purpose-less at the beginning of the Fifth Act. With masterly skill the poet here shows that what Durvasa's curse had brought about had its seeds in human nature.

In passing from the Fourth Act to the Fifth we suddenly enter a new atmosphere; from the ideal world of the hermitage we go forth to the royal court with its hard hearts, crooked ways of love-making, difficul-ties of union. The beauteous dream of the hermitage is about to be bro-ken. The two young hermits who are escorting Śakuntala, at once feel that they have entered an altogether different world, "a house encircled by fire!" By such touches at the beginning of the Fifth Act, the poet pre-pares us for the repudiation of Śakuntala at its end, lest the blow should be too severe for us.

Then comes the repudiation. Śakuntala feels as if she had been sud-denly struck with a thunderbolt. Like a deer stricken by a trusted hand, this daughter of the forest looks on in blank surprise, terror, and an-guish. At one blow she is hurled away from the hermitage, both literal and metaphorical, in which she has so long lived. She loses her con-nection with the loving friends, the birds, beasts, and plants, and the beauty, peace, and purity of her former life. She now stands alone, shel-terless. In one moment the music of the first four Acts is stilled!

O the deep silence and loneliness that then surround her! She whose tender heart has made the whole world of the hermitage her own folk, to-day stands absolutely alone. She fills this vast vacuity with her mighty sorrow. With rare poetic insight Kalidasa has declined to restore Śakuntala to Kanwa's hermitage. After the renunciation by Dushyanta it was impossible for her to live in harmony with that her-mitage in the way she had done before. . . . She was no longer her for-mer self; her relation with the universe had changed. Had she been placed again amidst her old surroundings, it would only have cruelly exhibited the utter inconsistency of the whole situation. A mighty si-lence was now needed, worthy of the mighty grief of the mourner. But the poet has not shown us the picture of Śakuntala in the new her-mitage—parted from the friends of her girlhood, and nursing the grief of separation from her lover. The silence of the poet only deepens our sense of the silence and vacancy which here reigned round Śakuntala. Had the repudiated wife been taken back to Kanwa's home, that her-mitage would have spoken. To our imagination its trees and creepers would have wept, the two girl friends would have mourned for Śakun-tala, even if the poet had not said a word about it. But in the unfamiliar hermitage of Marichi, all is still and silent to us; only we have before our mind's eye a picture of the world-abandoned Śakuntala's infinite sorrow, disciplined by penance, sedate, and resigned—seated like a recluse rapt in meditation.

Dushyanta is now consumed by remorse. This remorse is *tapaysa*. So long as Śakuntala was not won by means of this repentance, there was no glory in winning her. . . . One sudden gust of youthful impulse had in a moment given her up to Dushyanta, but that was not the true, the full winning of her. The best means of winning is by devotion, by *tapaysa*. What is easily gained is as easily lost. Therefore, the poet has made the two lovers undergo a long and austere *tapaysa* that they may gain each other truly eternally. If Dushyanta had accepted Śakuntala when she was first brought to his court, she would have only occupied a corner of the royal household, and passed the rest of her life in neglect, gloom, and uselessness.

It was a blessing in disguise for Śakuntala that Dushyanta abjured her with cruel sternness. When afterwards this cruelty reacted on himself, it prevented him from remaining indifferent to Śakuntala. His unceasing and intense grief fused his heart and welded Śakuntala with it. Never before had the King met with such an experience. Never before had he had the occasion and means of truly loving. Kings are unlucky in this respect; their desires are so easily satisfied that they never get what is to be gained by devotion alone. Fate now plunged Dushyanta into deep grief and thus made him worthy of true love—made him renounce the rôle of a rake.

Thus has Kalidasa burnt away vice in the eternal fire of the sinner's heart; he has not tried to conceal it from the outside. When the curtain drops in the last Act, we feel that all the evil has been destroyed as on a funeral pyre, and the peace born of a perfect and satisfactory fruition reigns in our hearts. Kalidasa has internally cut right away the roots of the poison tree, which a sudden force from the outside had planted. He has made the physical union of Dushyanta and Śakuntala tread the path of sorrow, and thereby chastened and sublimated it into a moral union. Hence did Goethe rightly say that *Śakuntala* combines the blossoms of Spring with the fruits of Autumn, it combines Heaven and Earth. Truly in *Śakuntala* there is one Paradise Lost and another Paradise Regained.

The poet has shown how the union of Dushyanta and Śakuntala in the First Act as mere lovers is futile, while their union in the last Act as the parents of Bharata is a true union. The First Act is full of brilliancy and movement. We have there a hermit's daughter in the exuberance of youth, her two companions running over with playfulness, the newly flowering forest creeper, the bee intoxicated with perfume, the

fascinated King peeping from behind the trees. From this Eden of bliss
Śakuntala, the mere sweetheart of Dushyanta, is exiled in disgrace. But
far different was the aspect of the other hermitage where Śakuntala, the
mother of Bharata and the incarnation of goodness took refuge. There
no hermit girls water the trees, nor bedew the creepers with their loving sister-like looks, nor feed the young fawn with handfuls of paddy.
There a single boy fills the loving bosom of the entire forest-world; he
absorbs all the liveliness of the trees, creepers, flowers, and foliage. The
matrons of the hermitage, in their loving anxiety, are fully taken up
with the unruly boy. When Śakuntala appears, we see her clad in a
dusty robe, face pale with austerities, doing the penance of a lorn wife,
pure-souled. Her long penances have purged her of the evil of her first
union with Dushyanta; she is now invested with the dignity of a ma-
tron, she is the image of motherhood, tender and good. Who can re-
pudiate her now?

The poet has shown here, as in *Kumara Sambhava*, that the Beauty
that goes hand in hand with Moral Law is eternal, that the calm, con-
trolled, and beneficent form of Love is its best form, that beauty is truly
charming under restraint and decays quickly when it gets wild and un-
fettered. This ancient poet of India refuses to recognise Love as its own
highest glory; he proclaims that Goodness is the final goal of Love. He
teaches us that the Love of man and woman is not beautiful, not last-
ing, not fruitful, so long as it is self-centred, so long as it does not beget
Goodness, so long as it does not diffuse itself into society over son and
daughter, guests and neighbours.

The two peculiar principles of India are the beneficent *tie of home
life* on the one hand, and the *liberty of the soul* abstracted from the
world on the other. In the world India is variously connected with
many races and many creeds; she cannot reject any of them. But on the
altar of devotion (*tapaysa*) India sits alone. Kalidasa has shown, both in
Śakuntala and *Kumara Sambhava*, that there is a harmony between
these two principles, an easy transition from the one to the other. In his
hermitage a human boy plays with lion cubs, and the hermit spirit is
reconciled with the spirit of the householder.

On the foundation of the hermitage of recluses Kalidasa has built
the home of the householder. He has rescued the relation of the sexes
from the sway of lust and enthroned it on the holy and pure seat of as-
ceticism. In the sacred books of the Hindus the ordered relation of the
sexes has been defined by strict injunctions and Laws. Kalidasa has
demonstrated *that* relation by means of the elements of Beauty. The
Beauty that he adores is lit up by grace, modesty, and goodness; in its
intensity it is true to one for ever; in its range it embraces the whole universe. It is fulfilled by renunciation, gratified by sorrow, and rendered

eternal by religion. In the midst of this beauty, the impetuous unruly love of man and woman has restrained itself and attained to a profound peace, like a wild torrent merged in the ocean of goodness. Therefore is such love higher and more wonderful than wild and untrained Passion.[1]

---

1. This article was originally written by the author in Bengali and was translated into English by Professor Jadunath Sarkar.

Contents

Dramatis Personæ

KING DUSHYANTA.
BHARATA, *nicknamed* All-tamer,
   his son.
MADHAVYA, *a clown, his compan-*
   ion.
His charioteer.
RAIVATAKA, *a door-keeper.*
BHADRASENA, *a general.*
KARABHAKA, *a servant.*
PARVATAYANA, *a chamberlain.*
SOMARATA, *a chaplain.*

KANVA, *hermit-father.*
SHARNGARAVA ⎱ *his pupils.*
SHARADVATA ⎰
HARITA
DURVASAS, *an irascible sage.*

The chief of police.
SUCHAKA ⎱ *policemen.*
JANUKA ⎰
A fisherman.

ŚAKUNTALA, *foster-child of Kanva.*
ANUSUYA ⎱ *her friends.*
PRIYAMVADA ⎰
GAUTAMI, *hermit-mother.*

KASHYAPA, *father of the gods.*
ADITI, *mother of the gods.*
MATALI, *charioteer of heaven's*
   king.
GALAVA, *a pupil in heaven.*
MISHRAKESHI, *a heavenly nymph.*

Stage-director and actress (in the prologue), hermits and hermit-
women, two court poets, palace attendants, invisible fairies.

The first four acts pass in Kanva's forest hermitage; acts five and six
in the king's palace; act seven on a heavenly mountain. The time is
perhaps seven years.

ŚAKUNTALA

PROLOGUE

BENEDICTION UPON THE AUDIENCE

Eight forms has Shiva, lord of all and king:
And these are water, first created thing;
And fire, which speeds the sacrifice begun;
The priest; and time's dividers, moon and sun;
The all-embracing ether, path of sound;
The earth, wherein all seeds of life are found;
And air, the breath of life: may he draw near,
Revealed in these, and bless those gathered here.

THE STAGE-DIRECTOR.   Enough of this! (*Turning toward the dressing-room.*) Madam, if you are ready, pray come here. (*Enter an actress.*)

ACTRESS.   Here I am, sir. What am I to do?

DIRECTOR.   Our audience is very discriminating, and we are to offer them a new play, called *Śakuntala and the ring of recognition,* written by the famous Kalidasa. Every member of the cast must be on his mettle.

ACTRESS.   Your arrangements are perfect. Nothing will go wrong.

DIRECTOR (*smiling*).   To tell the truth, madam,

> Until the wise are satisfied,
>   I cannot feel that skill is shown;
> The best-trained mind requires support,
>   And does not trust itself alone.

ACTRESS.   True. What shall we do first?

DIRECTOR.   First, you must sing something to please the ears of the audience.

ACTRESS.   What season of the year shall I sing about?

1

DIRECTOR.   Why, sing about the pleasant summer which has just begun. For at this time of year

> A mid-day plunge will temper heat;
>   The breeze is rich with forest flowers;
> To slumber in the shade is sweet;
>   And charming are the twilight hours.

ACTRESS (*sings*).

> The siris-blossoms fair,
>   With pollen laden,
> Are plucked to deck her hair
>   By many a maiden,
> But gently; flowers like these
> Are kissed by eager bees.

DIRECTOR.   Well done! The whole theatre is captivated by your song, and sits as if painted. What play shall we give them to keep their good-will?

ACTRESS.   Why, you just told me we were to give a new play called *Śakuntala and the ring*.

DIRECTOR.   Thank you for reminding me. For the moment I had quite forgotten.

> Your charming song had carried me away
> As the deer enticed the hero of our play.

> (*Exeunt ambo.*)

ACT I—THE HUNT

(Enter, in a chariot, pursuing a deer,
KING DUSHYANTA, *bow and arrow in hand; and a charioteer.)*

CHARIOTEER *(looking at the king and the deer).*   Your Majesty,

> I see you hunt the spotted deer
> With shafts to end his race,
>   As though God Shiva should appear
> In his immortal chase.

KING.   Charioteer, the deer has led us a long chase. And even now

> His neck in beauty bends
> As backward looks he sends
> At my pursuing car
> That threatens death from far.
> Fear shrinks to half the body small;
> See how he fears the arrow's fall!

> The path he takes is strewed
> With blades of grass half-chewed
> From jaws wide with the stress
> Of fevered weariness.
> He leaps so often and so high,
> He does not seem to run, but fly.

(In surprise.) Pursue as I may, I can hardly keep him in sight.

CHARIOTEER.   Your Majesty, I have been holding the horses back because the ground was rough. This checked us and gave the deer a lead. Now we are on level ground, and you will easily overtake him.

KING.   Then let the reins hang loose.

CHARIOTEER.   Yes, your Majesty. *(He counterfeits rapid motion.)* Look, your Majesty!

> The lines hang loose; the steeds unreined
>   Dart forward with a will.

Their ears are pricked; their necks are strained;
　　Their plumes lie straight and still.
They leave the rising dust behind;
They seem to float upon the wind.

KING (*joyfully*).　See! The horses are gaining on the deer.

As onward and onward the chariot flies,
The small flashes large to my dizzy eyes.
What is cleft in twain, seems to blur and mate;
What is crooked in nature, seems to be straight.
Things at my side in an instant appear
Distant, and things in the distance, near.

A VOICE BEHIND THE SCENES.　O King, this deer belongs to the hermitage, and must not be killed.

CHARIOTEER (*listening and looking*).　Your Majesty, here are two hermits, come to save the deer at the moment when your arrow was about to fall.

KING (*hastily*).　Stop the chariot.

CHARIOTEER.　Yes, your Majesty. (*He does so. Enter a hermit with his pupil.*)

HERMIT (*lifting his hand*).　O King, this deer belongs to the hermitage.

Why should his tender form expire,
As blossoms perish in the fire?
How could that gentle life endure
The deadly arrow, sharp and sure?

Restore your arrow to the quiver;
　　To you were weapons lent
The broken-hearted to deliver,
　　Not strike the innocent.

KING (*bowing low*).　It is done. (*He does so.*)

HERMIT (*joyfully*).　A deed worthy of you, scion of Puru's race, and shining example of kings. May you beget a son to rule earth and heaven.

KING (*bowing low*).　I am thankful for a Brahman's blessing.

THE TWO HERMITS.　O King, we are on our way to gather firewood. Here, along the bank of the Malini, you may see the hermitage of Father Kanva, over which Śakuntala presides, so to speak, as guardian deity. Unless other deities prevent, pray enter here and receive a welcome. Besides,

> Beholding pious hermit-rites
> Preserved from fearful harm,
> Perceive the profit of the scars
> On your protecting arm.

KING.   Is the hermit father there?

THE TWO HERMITS.   No, he has left his daughter to welcome guests, and has just gone to Somatirtha, to avert an evil fate that threatens her.

KING.   Well, I will see her. She shall feel my devotion, and report it to the sage.

THE TWO HERMITS.   Then we will go on our way. (*Exit hermit with pupil.*)

KING.   Charioteer, drive on. A sight of the pious hermitage will purify us.

CHARIOTEER.   Yes, your Majesty. (*He counterfeits motion again.*)

KING (*looking about*).   One would know, without being told, that this is the precinct of a pious grove.

CHARIOTEER.   How so?

KING.   Do you not see? Why, here

> Are rice-grains, dropped from bills of parrot chicks
> Beneath the trees; and pounding-stones where sticks
> A little almond-oil; and trustful deer
> That do not run away as we draw near;
> And river-paths that are besprinkled yet
> From trickling hermit-garments, clean and wet.

Besides,

> The roots of trees are washed by many a stream
> That breezes ruffle; and the flowers' red gleam
> Is dimmed by pious smoke; and fearless fawns
> Move softly on the close-cropped forest lawns.

CHARIOTEER.   It is all true.

KING (*after a little*).   We must not disturb the hermitage. Stop here while I dismount.

CHARIOTEER.   I am holding the reins. Dismount, your Majesty.

KING (*dismounts and looks at himself*).   One should wear modest garments on entering a hermitage. Take these jewels and the bow. (*He gives them to the charioteer.*) Before I return from my visit to the hermits, have the horses' backs wet down.

CHARIOTEER.   Yes, your Majesty. (*Exit.*)

KING (*walking and looking about*).   The hermitage! Well, I will enter. (*As he does so, he feels a throbbing in his arm.*)

> A tranquil spot! Why should I thrill?
> Love cannot enter there—
> Yet to inevitable things
> Doors open everywhere.

A VOICE BEHIND THE SCENES.   This way, girls!

KING (*listening*).   I think I hear some one to the right of the grove. I must find out. (*He walks and looks about.*) Ah, here are hermit-girls, with watering-pots just big enough for them to handle. They are coming in this direction to water the young trees. They are charming!

> The city maids, for all their pains,
> Seem not so sweet and good;
> Our garden blossoms yield to these
> Flower-children of the wood.

I will draw back into the shade and wait for them. (*He stands, gazing toward them. Enter* Śakuntala, *as described, and her two friends.*)

FIRST FRIEND.   It seems to me, dear, that Father Kanva cares more for the hermitage trees than he does for you. You are delicate as a jasmine blossom, yet he tells you to fill the trenches about the trees.

ŚAKUNTALA.   Oh, it isn't Father's bidding so much. I feel like a real sister to them. (*She waters the trees.*)

PRIYAMVADA.   Śakuntala, we have watered the trees that blossom in the summer-time. Now let's sprinkle those whose flowering-time is past. That will be a better deed, because we shall not be working for a reward.

ŚAKUNTALA.   What a pretty idea! (*She does so.*)

KING (*to himself*).   And this is Kanva's daughter, Śakuntala. (*In surprise.*) The good Father does wrong to make her wear the hermit's dress of bark.

> The sake who yokes her artless charm
> With pious pain and grief,
> Would try to cut the toughest vine
> With a soft, blue lotus-leaf.

Well, I will step behind a tree and see how she acts with her friends. (*He conceals himself.*)

ŚAKUNTALA.   Oh, Anusuya! Priyamvada has fastened this bark dress so tight that it hurts. Please loosen it. (*Anusuya does so.*)

PRIYAMVADA (*laughing*).   You had better blame your own budding charms for that.

KING.   She is quite right.

Beneath the barken dress
    Upon the shoulder tied,
In maiden loveliness
    Her young breast seems to hide,

As when a flower amid
    The leaves by autumn tossed—
Pale, withered leaves—lies hid,
    And half its grace is lost.

Yet in truth the bark dress is not an enemy to her beauty. It serves as an
added ornament. For

The meanest vesture glows
    On beauty that enchants:
The lotus lovelier shows
    Amid dull water-plants;

The moon in added splendour
    Shines for its spot of dark;
Yet more the maiden slender
    Charms in her dress of bark.

ŚAKUNTALA (*looking ahead*).   Oh, girls, that mango-tree is trying to
tell me something with his branches that move in the wind like fingers.
I must go and see him. (*She does so.*)

PRIYAMVADA.   There, Śakuntala, stand right where you are a
minute.

ŚAKUNTALA.   Why?

PRIYAMVADA.   When I see you there, it looks as if a vine were clinging to the mango-tree.

ŚAKUNTALA.   I see why they call you the flatterer.

KING.   But the flattery is true.

Her arms are tender shoots; her lips
    Are blossoms red and warm;
Bewitching youth begins to flower
    In beauty on her form.

ANUSUYA.   Oh, Śakuntala! Here is the jasmine-vine that you named
Light of the Grove. She has chosen the mango-tree as her husband.

ŚAKUNTALA (*approaches and looks at it, joyfully*).   What a pretty pair
they make. The jasmine shows her youth in her fresh flowers, and the
mango-tree shows his strength in his ripening fruit. (*She stands gazing
at them.*)

PRIYAMVADA (*smiling*).   Anusuya, do you know why Śakuntala looks so hard at the Light of the Grove?

ANUSUYA.   No. Why?

PRIYAMVADA.   She is thinking how the Light of the Grove has found a good tree, and hoping that she will meet a fine lover.

ŚAKUNTALA.   That's what you want for yourself. (*She tips her watering-pot.*)

ANUSUYA.   Look, Śakuntala! Here is the spring-creeper that Father Kanva tended with his own hands—just as he did you. You are forgetting her.

ŚAKUNTALA.   I'd forget myself sooner. (*She goes to the creeper and looks at it, joyfully.*) Wonderful! Wonderful! Priyamvada, I have something pleasant to tell you.

PRIYAMVADA.   What is it, dear?

ŚAKUNTALA.   It is out of season, but the spring-creeper is covered with buds down to the very root.

THE TWO FRIENDS (*running up*).   Really?

ŚAKUNTALA.   Of course. Can't you see?

PRIYAMVADA (*looking at it joyfully*).   And I have something pleasant to tell you. You are to be married soon.

ŚAKUNTALA (*snappishly*).   You know that's just what you want for yourself.

PRIYAMVADA.   I'm not teasing. I really heard Father Kanva say that this flowering vine was to be a symbol of your coming happiness.

ANUSUYA.   Priyamvada, that is why Śakuntala waters the spring-creeper so lovingly.

ŚAKUNTALA.   She is my sister. Why shouldn't I give her water? (*She tips her watering-pot.*)

KING.   May I hope that she is the hermit's daughter by a mother of a different caste? But it *must* be so.

> Surely, she may become a warrior's bride;
>   Else, why these longings in an honest mind?
> The motions of a blameless heart decide
>   Of right and wrong, when reason leaves us blind.

Yet I will learn the whole truth.

ŚAKUNTALA (*excitedly*).   Oh, oh! A bee has left the jasmine-vine and is flying into my face. (*She shows herself annoyed by the bee.*)

KING (*ardently*).

> As the bee about her flies,
> Swiftly her bewitching eyes
>   Turn to watch his flight.
> She is practising to-day

Coquetry and glances' play
　　Not from love, but fright.

(*Jealously.*)

Eager bee, you lightly skim
O'er the eyelid's trembling rim
　　Toward the cheek aquiver.
Gently buzzing round her cheek,
Whispering in her ear, you seek
　　Secrets to deliver.

While her hands that way and this
Strike at you, you steal a kiss,
　　Love's all, honeymaker.
I know nothing but her name,
Not her caste, nor whence she came—
　　You, my rival, take her.

ŚAKUNTALA.   Oh, girls! Save me from this dreadful bee!
THE TWO FRIENDS (*smiling*).   Who are we, that we should save you?
Call upon Dushyanta. For pious groves are in the protection of the
king.
KING.   A good opportunity to present myself. Have no— (*He checks
himself. Aside.*) No, they would see that I am the king. I prefer to ap-
pear as a guest.
ŚAKUNTALA.   He doesn't leave me alone! I am going to run away.
(*She takes a step and looks about.*) Oh, dear! Oh, dear! He is following
me. Please save me.
KING (*hastening forward*).   Ah!

A king of Puru's mighty line
　　Chastises shameless churls;
What insolent is he who baits
　　These artless hermit-girls?

(*The girls are a little flurried on seeing the king.*)
ANUSUYA.   It is nothing very dreadful, sir. But our friend (*indicating*
ŚAKUNTALA) was teased and frightened by a bee.
KING (*to* ŚAKUNTALA).   I hope these pious days are happy ones.
(ŚAKUNTALA's *eyes drop in embarrassment.*)
ANUSUYA.   Yes, now that we receive such a distinguished guest.
PRIYAMVADA.   Welcome, sir. Go to the cottage, Śakuntala, and bring
fruit. This water will do to wash the feet.
KING.   Your courteous words are enough to make me feel at home.
ANUSUYA.   Then, sir, pray sit down and rest on this shady bench.

KING. You, too, are surely wearied by your pious task. Pray be seated a moment.

PRIYAMVADA (*aside to* ŚAKUNTALA). My dear, we must be polite to our guest. Shall we sit down? (*The three girls sit.*)

ŚAKUNTALA (*to herself*). Oh, why do I have such feelings when I see this man? They seem wrong in a hermitage.

KING (*looking at the girls*). It is delightful to see your friendship. For you are all young and beautiful.

PRIYAMVADA (*aside to* ANUSUYA). Who is he, dear? With his mystery, and his dignity, and his courtesy? He acts like a king and a gentleman.

ANUSUYA. I am curious too. I am going to ask him. (*Aloud.*) Sir, you are so very courteous that I make bold to ask you something. What royal family do you adorn, sir? What country is grieving at your absence? Why does a gentleman so delicately bred submit to the weary journey into our pious grove?

ŚAKUNTALA (*aside*). Be brave, my heart. Anusuya speaks your very thoughts.

KING (*aside*). Shall I tell at once who I am, or conceal it? (*He reflects.*) This will do. (*Aloud.*) I am a student of Scripture. It is my duty to see justice done in the cities of the king. And I have come to this hermitage on a tour of inspection.

ANUSUYA. Then we of the hermitage have some one to take care of us. (ŚAKUNTALA *shows embarrassment.*)

THE TWO FRIENDS (*observing the demeanour of the pair. Aside to* ŚAKUNTALA). Oh, Śakuntala! If only Father were here to-day.

ŚAKUNTALA. What would he do?

THE TWO FRIENDS. He would make our distinguished guest happy, if it took his most precious treasure.

ŚAKUNTALA (*feigning anger*). Go away! You mean something. I'll not listen to you.

KING. I too would like to ask a question about your friend.

THE TWO FRIENDS. Sir, your request is a favour to us.

KING. Father Kanva lives a lifelong hermit. Yet you say that your friend is his daughter. How can that be?

ANUSUYA. Listen, sir. There is a majestic royal sage named Kaushika——

KING. Ah, yes. The famous Kaushika.

ANUSUYA. Know, then, that he is the source of our friend's being. But Father Kanva is her real father, because he took care of her when she was abandoned.

KING. You waken my curiosity with the word "abandoned." May I hear the whole story?

ANUSUYA.   Listen, sir. Many years ago, that royal sage was leading a life of stern austerities, and the gods, becoming strangely jealous, sent the nymph Menaka to disturb his devotions.

KING.   Yes, the gods feel this jealousy toward the austerities of others. And then——

ANUSUYA.   Then in the lovely spring-time he saw her intoxicating beauty—— (*She stops in embarrassment.*)

KING.   The rest is plain. Surely, she is the daughter of the nymph.

ANUSUYA.   Yes.

KING.   It is as it should be.

> To beauty such as this
>   No woman could give birth;
> The quivering lightning flash
>   Is not a child of earth.

(ŚAKUNTALA *hangs her head in confusion.*)

KING (*to himself*).   Ah, my wishes become hopes.

PRIYAMVADA (*looking with a smile at* ŚAKUNTALA).   Sir, it seems as if you had more to say. (ŚAKUNTALA *threatens her friend with her finger.*)

KING.   You are right. Your pious life interests me, and I have another question.

PRIYAMVADA.   Do not hesitate. We hermit people stand ready to answer all demands.

KING.   My question is this:

> Does she, till marriage only, keep her vow
>   As hermit-maid, that shames the ways of love?
> Or must her soft eyes ever see, as now,
>   Soft eyes of friendly deer in peaceful grove?

PRIYAMVADA.   Sir, we are under bonds to lead a life of virtue. But it is her father's wish to give her to a suitable lover.

KING (*joyfully to himself*).

> O heart, your wish is won!
> All doubt at last is done;
> The thing you feared as fire,
> Is the jewel of your desire.

ŚAKUNTALA (*pettishly*).   Anusuya, I'm going.

ANUSUYA.   What for?

ŚAKUNTALA.   I am going to tell Mother Gautami that Priyamvada is talking nonsense. (*She rises.*)

ANUSUYA.   My dear, we hermit people cannot neglect to entertain a distinguished guest, and go wandering about.

(ŚAKUNTALA *starts to walk away without answering.*)

KING (*aside*).　She is going! (*He starts up as if to detain her, then checks his desires.*) A thought is as vivid as an act, to a lover.

> Though nurture, conquering nature, holds
> 　　Me back, it seems
> As had I started and returned
> 　　In waking dreams.

PRIYAMVADA (*approaching* ŚAKUNTALA).　You dear, peevish girl! You mustn't go.

ŚAKUNTALA (*turns with a frown*).　Why not?

PRIYAMVADA.　You owe me the watering of two trees. You can go when you have paid your debt. (*She forces her to come back.*)

KING.　It is plain that she is already wearied by watering the trees. See!

> Her shoulders droop; her palms are reddened yet;
> 　　Quick breaths are struggling in her bosom fair;
> The blossom o'er her ear hangs limply wet;
> 　　One hand restrains the loose, dishevelled hair.

I therefore remit her debt. (*He gives the two friends a ring. They take it, read the name engraved on it, and look at each other.*)

KING.　Make no mistake. This is a present—from the king.

PRIYAMVADA.　Then, sir, you ought not to part with it. Your word is enough to remit the debt.

ANUSUYA.　Well, Śakuntala, you are set free by this kind gentleman—or rather, by the king himself. Where are you going now?

ŚAKUNTALA (*to herself*).　I would never leave him if I could help myself.

PRIYAMVADA.　Why don't you go now?

ŚAKUNTALA.　I am not *your* servant any longer. I will go when I like.

KING (*looking at* ŚAKUNTALA. *To himself*).　Does she feel toward me as I do toward her? At least, there is ground for hope.

> Although she does not speak to me,
> 　　She listens while I speak;
> Her eyes turn not to see my face,
> 　　But nothing else they seek.

A VOICE BEHIND THE SCENES.　Hermits! Hermits! Prepare to defend the creatures in our pious grove. King Dushyanta is hunting in the neighbourhood.

> The dust his horses' hoofs have raised,

> Red as the evening sky,
>   Falls like a locust-swarm on boughs
>   Where hanging garments dry.

KING (*aside*).   Alas! My soldiers are disturbing the pious grove in their search for me.

THE VOICE BEHIND THE SCENES.   Hermits! Hermits! Here is an elephant who is terrifying old men, women, and children.

> One tusk is splintered by a cruel blow
> Against a blocking tree; his gait is slow,
>   For countless fettering vines impede and cling;
> He puts the deer to flight; some evil thing
> He seems, that comes our peaceful life to mar,
>   Fleeing in terror from the royal car.

(*The girls listen and rise anxiously.*)

KING.   I have offended sadly against the hermits. I must go back.

THE TWO FRIENDS.   Your Honour, we are frightened by this alarm of the elephant. Permit us to return to the cottage.

ANUSUYA (*to* ŚAKUNTALA).   Śakuntala dear, Mother Gautami will be anxious. We must hurry and find her.

ŚAKUNTALA (*feigning lameness*).   Oh, oh! I can hardly walk.

KING.   You must go very slowly. And I will take pains that the hermitage is not disturbed.

THE TWO FRIENDS.   Your honour, we feel as if we knew you very well. Pray pardon our shortcomings as hostesses. May we ask you to seek better entertainment from us another time?

KING.   You are too modest. I feel honoured by the mere sight of you.

ŚAKUNTALA.   Anusuya, my foot is cut on a sharp blade of grass, and my dress is caught on an amaranth twig. Wait for me while I loosen it. (*She casts a lingering glance at the king, and goes out with her two friends.*)

KING (*sighing*).   They are gone. And I must go. The sight of Śakuntala has made me dread the return to the city. I will make my men camp at a distance from the pious grove. But I cannot turn my own thoughts from Śakuntala.

> It is my body leaves my love, not I;
>   My body moves away, but not my mind;
> For back to her my struggling fancies fly
>   Like silken banners borne against the wind.

(*Exit.*)

ACT II — THE SECRET

(Enter the clown.)

CLOWN (*sighing*).   Damn! Damn! Damn! I'm tired of being friends with this sporting king. "There's a deer!" he shouts, "There's a boar!" And off he chases on a summer noon through woods where shade is few and far between. We drink hot, stinking water from the mountain streams, flavoured with leaves—nasty! At odd times we get a little tepid meat to eat. And the horses and the elephants make such a noise that I can't even be comfortable at night. Then the hunters and the bird-chasers—damn 'em—wake me up bright and early. They do make an ear-splitting rumpus when they start for the woods. But even that isn't the whole misery. There's a new pimple growing on the old boil. He left us behind and went hunting a deer. And there in a hermitage they say he found—oh, dear! oh, dear! he found a hermit-girl named Śakuntala. Since then he hasn't a thought of going back to town. I lay awake all night, thinking about it. What can I do? Well, I'll see my friend when he is dressed and beautified. (*He walks and looks about.*) Hello! Here he comes, with his bow in his hand, and his girl in his heart. He is wearing a wreath of wild flowers! I'll pretend to be all knocked up. Perhaps I can get a rest that way. (*He stands, leaning on his staff. Enter the king, as described.*)

KING (*to himself*).

> Although my darling is not lightly won,
>> She seemed to love me, and my hopes are bright;
> Though love be balked ere joy be well begun,
>> A common longing is itself delight.

(*Smiling.*) Thus does a lover deceive himself. He judges his love's feelings by his own desires.

> Her glance was loving—but 'twas not for me;
> Her step was slow—'twas grace, not coquetry;
> Her speech was short—to her detaining friend.
> In things like these love reads a selfish end!

14

CLOWN (*standing as before*).   Well, king, I can't move my hand. I can only greet you with my voice.

KING (*looking and smiling*).   What makes you lame?

CLOWN.   Good! You hit a man in the eye, and then ask him why the tears come.

KING.   I do not understand you. Speak plainly.

CLOWN.   When a reed bends over like a hunchback, do you blame the reed or the river-current?

KING.   The river-current, of course.

CLOWN.   And you are to blame for my troubles.

KING.   How so?

CLOWN.   It's a fine thing for you to neglect your royal duties and such a sure job—to live in the woods! What's the good of talking? Here I am, a Brahman, and my joints are all shaken up by this eternal running after wild animals, so that I can't move. Please be good to me. Let us have a rest for just one day.

KING (*to himself*).   He says this. And I too, when I remember Kanva's daughter, have little desire for the chase. For

> The bow is strung, its arrow near;
> > And yet I cannot bend
> That bow against the fawns who share
> > Soft glances with their friend.

CLOWN (*observing the king*).   He means more than he says. I might as well weep in the woods.

KING (*smiling*).   What more could I mean? I have been thinking that I ought to take my friend's advice.

CLOWN (*cheerfully*).   Long life to you, then. (*He unstiffens.*)

KING.   Wait. Hear me out.

CLOWN.   Well, sir?

KING.   When you are rested, you must be my companion in another task—an easy one.

CLOWN.   Crushing a few sweetmeats?

KING.   I will tell you presently.

CLOWN.   Pray command my leisure.

KING.   Who stands without? (*Enter the door-keeper.*)

DOOR-KEEPER.   I await your Majesty's commands.

KING.   Raivataka, summon the general.

DOOR-KEEPER.   Yes, your Majesty. (*He goes out, then returns with the general.*) Follow me, sir. There is his Majesty, listening to our conversation. Draw near, sir.

GENERAL (*observing the king, to himself*).   Hunting is declared to be a sin, yet it brings nothing but good to the king. See!

He does not heed the cruel sting
Of his recoiling, twanging string;
The mid-day sun, the dripping sweat
Affect him not, nor make him fret;
His form, though sinewy and spare,
Is most symmetrically fair;
No mountain-elephant could be
More filled with vital strength than he.

(*He approaches.*) Victory to your Majesty! The forest is full of deer-tracks, and beasts of prey cannot be far off. What better occupation could we have?

KING.   Bhadrasena, my enthusiasm is broken. Madhavya has been preaching against hunting.

GENERAL (*aside to the clown*).   Stick to it, friend Madhavya. I will humour the king a moment. (*Aloud.*) Your Majesty, he is a chattering idiot. Your Majesty may judge by his own case whether hunting is an evil. Consider:

The hunter's form grows sinewy, strong, and light;
He learns, from beasts of prey, how wrath and fright
Affect the mind; his skill he loves to measure
With moving targets. 'Tis life's chiefest pleasure.

CLOWN (*angrily*).   Get out! Get out with your strenuous life! The king has come to his senses. But you, you son of a slave-wench, can go chasing from forest to forest, till you fall into the jaws of some old bear that is looking for a deer or a jackal.

KING.   Bhadrasena, I cannot take your advice, because I am in the vicinity of a hermitage. So for to-day

The hornèd buffalo may shake
The turbid water of the lake;
Shade-seeking deer may chew the cud,
Boars trample swamp-grass in the mud;
The bow I bend in hunting, may
Enjoy a listless holiday.

GENERAL.   Yes, your Majesty.

KING.   Send back the archers who have gone ahead. And forbid the soldiers to vex the hermitage, or even to approach it. Remember:

There lurks a hidden fire in each
    Religious hermit-bower;
Cool sun-stones kindle if assailed
    By any foreign power.

GENERAL.   Yes, your Majesty.

CLOWN.   Now will you get out with your strenuous life? (*Exit general.*)

KING (*to his attendants*).   Lay aside your hunting dress. And you, Raivataka, return to your post of duty.

RAIVATAKA.   Yes, your Majesty. (*Exit.*)

CLOWN.   You have got rid of the vermin. Now be seated on this flat stone, over which the trees spread their canopy of shade. I can't sit down till you do.

KING.   Lead the way.

CLOWN.   Follow me. (*They walk about and sit down.*)

KING.   Friend Madhavya, you do not know what vision is. You have not seen the fairest of all objects.

CLOWN.   I see you, right in front of me.

KING.   Yes, every one thinks himself beautiful. But I was speaking of Śakuntala, the ornament of the hermitage.

CLOWN (*to himself*).   I mustn't add fuel to the flame. (*Aloud.*) But you can't have her because she is a hermit-girl. What is the use of seeing her?

KING.   Fool!

> And is it selfish longing then,
>   That draws our souls on high
> Through eyes that have forgot to wink,
>   As the new moon climbs the sky?

Besides, Dushyanta's thoughts dwell on no forbidden object.

CLOWN.   Well, tell me about her.

KING.

> Sprung from a nymph of heaven
>   Wanton and gay,
> Who spurned the blessing given,
>   Going her way;
>
> By the stern hermit taken
>   In her most need:
> So fell the blossom shaken,
>   Flower on a weed.

CLOWN (*laughing*).   You are like a man who gets tired of good dates and longs for sour tamarind. All the pearls of the palace are yours, and you want this girl!

KING.   My friend, you have not seen her, or you could not talk so.

CLOWN.   She must be charming if she surprises *you*.

KING.   Oh, my friend, she needs not many words.

> She is God's vision, of pure thought
>   Composed in His creative mind;
> His reveries of beauty wrought
>   The peerless pearl of womankind.
> So plays my fancy when I see
> How great is God, how lovely she.

CLOWN.   How the women must hate her!
KING.   This too is in my thought.

> She seems a flower whose fragrance none has tasted,
>   A gem uncut by workman's tool,
> A branch no desecrating hands have wasted,
>   Fresh honey, beautifully cool.

> No man on earth deserves to taste her beauty,
>   Her blameless loveliness and worth,
> Unless he has fulfilled man's perfect duty—
>   And is there such a one on earth?

CLOWN.   Marry her quick, then, before the poor girl falls into the hands of some oily-headed hermit.
KING.   She is dependent on her father, and he is not here.
CLOWN.   But how does she feel toward you?
KING.   My friend, hermit-girls are by their very nature timid. And yet

> When I was near, she could not look at me;
>   She smiled—but not to me—and half denied it;
> She would not show her love for modesty,
>   Yet did not try so very hard to hide it.

CLOWN.   Did you want her to climb into your lap the first time she saw you?
KING.   But when she went away with her friends, she almost showed that she loved me.

> When she had hardly left my side,
>   "I cannot walk," the maiden cried,
> And turned her face, and feigned to free
> The dress not caught upon the tree.

CLOWN.   She has given you some memories to chew on. I suppose that is why you are so in love with the pious grove.
KING.   My friend, think of some pretext under which we may return to the hermitage.

CLOWN.   What pretext do you need? Aren't you the king?
KING.   What of that?
CLOWN.   Collect the taxes on the hermits' rice.
KING.   Fool! It is a very different tax which these hermits pay—one that outweighs heaps of gems.

> The wealth we take from common men,
>   Wastes while we cherish;
> These share with us such holiness
>   As ne'er can perish.

VOICES BEHIND THE SCENES.   Ah, we have found him.
KING (*listening*).   The voices are grave and tranquil. These must be hermits. (*Enter the door-keeper.*)
DOOR-KEEPER.   Victory, O King. There are two hermit-youths at the gate.
KING.   Bid them enter at once.
DOOR-KEEPER.   Yes, your Majesty. (*He goes out, then returns with the youths.*) Follow me.
FIRST YOUTH (*looking at the king*).   A majestic presence, yet it inspires confidence. Nor is this wonderful in a king who is half a saint. For to him

> The splendid palace serves as hermitage;
> His royal government, courageous, sage,
> Adds daily to his merit; it is given
> To him to win applause from choirs of heaven
> Whose anthems to his glory rise and swell,
> Proclaiming him a king, and saint as well.

SECOND YOUTH.   My friend, is this Dushyanta, friend of Indra?
FIRST YOUTH.   It is.
SECOND YOUTH.

> Nor is it wonderful that one whose arm
> Might bolt a city gate, should keep from harm
>   The whole broad earth dark-belted by the sea;
> For when the gods in heaven with demons fight,
> Dushyanta's bow and Indra's weapon bright
>   Are their reliance for the victory.

THE TWO YOUTHS (*approaching*).   Victory, O King!
KING (*rising*).   I salute you.
THE TWO YOUTHS.   All hail! (*They offer fruit.*)
KING (*receiving it and bowing low*).   May I know the reason of your coming?

THE TWO YOUTHS. The hermits have learned that you are here, and they request——

KING. They command rather.

THE TWO YOUTHS. The powers of evil disturb our pious life in the absence of the hermit-father. We therefore ask that you will remain a few nights with your charioteer to protect the hermitage.

KING. I shall be most happy to do so.

CLOWN (*to the king*). You rather seem to like being collared this way.

KING. Raivataka, tell my charioteer to drive up, and to bring the bow and arrows.

RAIVATAKA. Yes, your Majesty. (*Exit.*)

THE TWO YOUTHS.

> Thou art a worthy scion of
> The kings who ruled our nation
> And found, defending those in need,
> Their truest consecration.

KING. Pray go before. And I will follow straightway.

THE TWO YOUTHS. Victory, O King! (*Exeunt.*)

KING. Madhavya, have you no curiosity to see Sakuntala?

CLOWN. I *did* have an unending curiosity, but this talk about the powers of evil has put an end to it.

KING. Do not fear. You will be with me.

CLOWN. I'll stick close to your chariot-wheel. (*Enter the door-keeper.*)

DOOR-KEEPER. Your Majesty, the chariot is ready, and awaits your departure to victory. But one Karabhaka has come from the city, a messenger from the queen-mother.

KING (*respectfully*). Sent by my mother?

DOOR-KEEPER. Yes.

KING. Let him enter.

DOOR-KEEPER (*goes out and returns with* KARABHAKA). Karabhaka, here is his Majesty. You may draw near.

KARABHAKA (*approaching and bowing low*). Victory to your Majesty. The queen-mother sends her commands——

KING. What are her commands?

KARABHAKA. She plans to end a fasting ceremony on the fourth day from to-day. And on that occasion her dear son must not fail to wait upon her.

KING. On the one side is my duty to the hermits, on the other my mother's command. Neither may be disregarded. What is to be done?

CLOWN (*laughing*). Stay half-way between, like Trishanku.

KING.   In truth, I am perplexed.

> Two inconsistent duties sever
>   My mind with cruel shock,
> As when the current of a river
>   Is split upon a rock.

(*He reflects.*) My friend, the queen-mother has always felt toward you as toward a son. Do you return, tell her what duty keeps me here, and yourself perform the offices of a son.

CLOWN.   You don't think I am afraid of the devils?

KING (*smiling*).   O mighty Brahman, who could suspect it?

CLOWN.   But I want to travel like a prince.

KING.   I will send all the soldiers with you, for the pious grove must not be disturbed.

CLOWN (*strutting*).   Aha! Look at the heir-apparent!

KING (*to himself*).   The fellow is a chatterbox. He might betray my longing to the ladies of the palace. Good, then! (*He takes the clown by the hand. Aloud.*) Friend Madhavya, my reverence for the hermits draws me to the hermitage. Do not think that I am really in love with the hermit-girl. Just think:

> A king, and a girl of the calm hermit-grove,
> Bred with the fawns, and a stranger to love!
> Then do not imagine a serious quest;
> The light words I uttered were spoken in jest.

CLOWN.   Oh, I understand that well enough.

(Exeunt ambo.)

ACT III — THE LOVE-MAKING

(Enter a pupil, with sacred grass for the sacrifice.)

PUPIL (*with meditative astonishment*).   How great is the power of King Dushyanta! Since his arrival our rites have been undisturbed.

> He does not need to bend the bow;
> For every evil thing,
> Awaiting not the arrow, flees
> From the twanging of the string.

Well, I will take this sacred grass to the priests, to strew the altar. (*He walks and looks about, then speaks to some one not visible.*) Priyamvada, for whom are you carrying this cuscus-salve and the fibrous lotus-leaves? (*He listens.*) What do you say? That Śakuntala has become seriously ill from the heat, and that these things are to relieve her suffering? Give her the best of care, Priyamvada. She is the very life of the hermit-father. And I will give Gautami the holy water for her. (*Exit. Enter the lovelorn king.*)

KING (*with a meditative sigh*).

> I know that stern religion's power
> Keeps guardian watch my maiden o'er;
> Yet all my heart flows straight to her
> Like water to the valley-floor.

Oh, mighty Love, thine arrows are made of flowers. How can they be so sharp? (*He recalls something.*) Ah, I understand.

> Shiva's devouring wrath still burns in thee,
> As burns the eternal fire beneath the sea;
>   Else how couldst thou, thyself long since consumed,
> Kindle the fire that flames so ruthlessly?

Indeed, the moon and thou inspire confidence, only to deceive the host of lovers.

> Thy shafts are blossoms; coolness streams
> From moon-rays: thus the poets sing;
> But to the lovelorn, falsehood seems
> To lurk in such imagining;
> The moon darts fire from frosty beams;
> Thy flowery arrows cut and sting.

And yet

> If Love will trouble her
> Whose great eyes madden me,
> I greet him unafraid,
> Though wounded ceaselessly.

O mighty god, wilt thou not show me mercy after such reproaches?

> With tenderness unending
> I cherished thee when small,
> In vain—thy bow is bending;
> On me thine arrows fall.
> My care for thee to such a plight
> Has brought me; and it serves me right.

I have driven off the powers of evil, and the hermits have dismissed me. Where shall I go now to rest from my weariness? (*He sighs.*) There is no rest for me except in seeing her whom I love. (*He looks up.*) She usually spends these hours of midday heat with her friends on the vine-wreathed banks of the Malini. I will go there. (*He walks and looks about.*) I believe the slender maiden has just passed through this corridor of young trees. For

> The stems from which the gathered flowers
> Are still unhealed;
> The sap where twigs were broken off
> Is uncongealed.

(*He feels a breeze stirring.*) This is a pleasant spot, with the wind among the trees.

> Limbs that love's fever seizes,
> Their fervent welcome pay
> To lotus-fragrant breezes
> That bear the river-spray.

(*He studies the ground.*) Ah, Śakuntala must be in this reedy bower. For

> In white sand at the door
> Fresh footprints appear,

> The toe lightly outlined,
> The heel deep and clear.

I will hide among the branches, and see what happens. (*He does so. Joyfully.*) Ah, my eyes have found their heaven. Here is the darling of my thoughts, lying upon a flower-strewn bench of stone, and attended by her two friends. I will hear what they say to each other. (*He stands gazing. Enter* ŚAKUNTALA *with her two friends.*)

THE TWO FRIENDS (*fanning her*). Do you feel better, dear, when we fan you with these lotus-leaves?

ŚAKUNTALA (*wearily*). Oh, are you fanning me, my dear girls? (*The two friends look sorrowfully at each other.*)

KING. She is seriously ill. (*Doubtfully.*) Is it the heat, or is it as I hope? (*Decidedly.*) It *must* be so.

> With salve upon her breast,
> With loosened lotus-chain,
> My darling, sore oppressed,
> Is lovely in her pain.

> Though love and summer heat
> May work an equal woe,
> No maiden seems so sweet
> When summer lays her low.

PRIYAMVADA (*aside to* ANUSUYA). Anusuya, since she first saw the good king, she has been greatly troubled. I do not believe her fever has any other cause.

ANUSUYA. I suspect you are right. I am going to ask her. My dear, I must ask you something. You are in a high fever.

KING. It is too true.

> Her lotus-chains that were as white
> As moonbeams shining in the night,
> Betray the fever's awful pain,
> And fading, show a darker stain.

ŚAKUNTALA (*half rising*). Well, say whatever you like.

ANUSUYA. Śakuntala dear, you have not told us what is going on in your mind. But I have heard old, romantic stories, and I can't help thinking that you are in a state like that of a lady in love. Please tell us what hurts you. We have to understand the disease before we can even try to cure it.

KING. Anusuya expresses my own thoughts.

ŚAKUNTALA. It hurts me terribly. I can't tell you all at once.

PRIYAMVADA. Anusuya is right, dear. Why do you hide your trouble?

You are wasting away every day. You are nothing but a beautiful shadow.

KING.   Priyamvada is right. See!

> Her cheeks grow thin; her breast and shoulders fail;
> Her waist is weary and her face is pale:
> She fades for love; oh, pitifully sweet!
> As vine-leaves wither in the scorching heat.

ŚAKUNTALĀ (*sighing*).   I could not tell any one else. But I shall be a burden to you.

THE TWO FRIENDS.   That is why we insist on knowing, dear. Grief must be shared to be endured.

KING.

> To friends who share her joy and grief
> She tells what sorrow laid her here;
> She turned to look her love again
> When first I saw her—yet I fear!

ŚAKUNTALĀ.   Ever since I saw the good king who protects the pious grove—— (*She stops and fidgets.*)

THE TWO FRIENDS.   Go on, dear.

ŚAKUNTALĀ.   I love him, and it makes me feel like this.

THE TWO FRIENDS.   Good, good! You have found a lover worthy of your devotion. But of course, a great river always runs into the sea.

KING (*joyfully*).   I have heard what I longed to hear.

> 'Twas love that caused the burning pain;
> 'Tis love that eases it again;
> As when, upon a sultry day,
> Rain breaks, and washes grief away.

ŚAKUNTALĀ.   Then, if you think best, make the good king take pity upon me. If not, remember that I was.

KING.   Her words end all doubt.

PRIYAMVADA (*aside to* ANUSUYA).   Anusuya, she is far gone in love and cannot endure any delay.

ANUSUYA.   Priyamvada, can you think of any scheme by which we could carry out her wishes quickly and secretly?

PRIYAMVADA.   We must plan about the "secretly." The "quickly" is not hard.

ANUSUYA.   How so?

PRIYAMVADA.   Why, the good king shows his love for her in his tender glances, and he has been wasting away, as if he were losing sleep.

KING.   It is quite true.

> The hot tears, flowing down my cheek
>   All night on my supporting arm
> And on its golden bracelet, seek
>   To stain the gems and do them harm.

> The bracelet slipping o'er the scars
>   Upon the wasted arm, that show
> My deeds in hunting and in wars,
>   All night is moving to and fro.

PRIYAMVADA (*reflecting*).   Well, she must write him a love-letter. And I will hide it in a bunch of flowers and see that it gets into the king's hand as if it were a relic of the sacrifice.

ANUSUYA.   It is a pretty plan, dear, and it pleases me. What does Śakuntala say?

ŚAKUNTALA.   I suppose I must obey orders.

PRIYAMVADA.   Then compose a pretty little love-song, with a hint of yourself in it.

ŚAKUNTALA.   I'll try. But my heart trembles, for fear he will despise me.

KING.

> Here stands the eager lover, and you pale
>   For fear lest he disdain a love so kind:
> The seeker may find fortune, or may fail;
>   But how could fortune, seeking, fail to find?

And again:

> The ardent lover comes, and yet you fear
>   Lest he disdain love's tribute, were it brought,
> The hope of which has led his footsteps here—
>   Pearls need not seek, for they themselves are sought.

THE TWO FRIENDS.   You are too modest about your own charms. Would anybody put up a parasol to keep off the soothing autumn moonlight?

ŚAKUNTALA (*smiling*).   I suppose I shall have to obey orders. (*She meditates.*)

KING.   It is only natural that I should forget to wink when I see my darling. For

> One clinging eyebrow lifted,
>   As fitting words she seeks,
> Her face reveals her passion
>   For me in glowing cheeks.

Śakuntala.   Well, I have thought out a little song. But I haven't anything to write with.

Priyamvada.   Here is a lotus-leaf, glossy as a parrot's breast. You can cut the letters in it with your nails.

Śakuntala.   Now listen, and tell me whether it makes sense.

The two friends.   Please.

Śakuntala (*reads*).

> I know not if I read your heart aright;
>   Why, pitiless, do you distress me so?
> I only know that longing day and night
>   Tosses my restless body to and fro,
>   That yearns for you, the source of all its woe.

King (*advancing*).

> Though Love torments you, slender maid,
>   Yet he consumes me quite,
> As daylight shuts night-blooming flowers
>   And slays the moon outright.

The two friends (*perceive the king and rise joyfully*).   Welcome to the wish that is fulfilled without delay. (Śakuntala *tries to rise.*)

King.   Do not try to rise, beautiful Śakuntala.

> Your limbs from which the strength is fled,
> That crush the blossoms of your bed
> And bruise the lotus-leaves, may be
> Pardoned a breach of courtesy.

Śakuntala (*sadly to herself*).   Oh, my heart, you were so impatient, and now you find no answer to make.

Anusuya.   Your Majesty, pray do this stone bench the honour of sitting upon it. (Śakuntala *edges away.*)

King (*seating himself*).   Priyamvada, I trust your friend's illness is not dangerous.

Priyamvada (*smiling*).   A remedy is being applied and it will soon be better. It is plain, sir, that you and she love each other. But I love her too, and I must say something over again.

King.   Pray do not hesitate. It always causes pain in the end, to leave unsaid what one longs to say.

Priyamvada.   Then listen, sir.

King.   I am all attention.

Priyamvada.   It is the king's duty to save hermit-folk from all suffering. Is not that good Scripture?

King.   There is no text more urgent.

PRIYAMVADA. Well, our friend has been brought to this sad state by her love for you. Will you not take pity on her and save her life?

KING. We cherish the same desire. I feel it a great honour.

ŚAKUNTALA (*with a jealous smile*). Oh, don't detain the good king. He is separated from the court ladies, and he is anxious to go back to them.

KING.

> Bewitching eyes that found my heart,
>   You surely see
> It could no longer live apart,
>   Nor faithless be.
> I bear Love's arrows as I can;
> Wound not with doubt a wounded man.

ANUSUYA. But, your Majesty, we hear that kings have many favourites. You must act in such a way that our friend may not become a cause of grief to her family.

KING. What more can I say?

> Though many queens divide my court,
>   But two support the throne;
> Your friend will find a rival in
>   The sea-girt earth alone.

THE TWO FRIENDS. We are content. (ŚAKUNTALA *betrays her joy.*)

PRIYAMVADA (*aside to* ANUSUYA). Look, Anusuya! See how the dear girl's life is coming back moment by moment—just like a peahen in summer when the first rainy breezes come.

ŚAKUNTALA. You must please ask the king's pardon for the rude things we said when we were talking together.

THE TWO FRIENDS (*smiling*). Anybody who says it was rude, may ask his pardon. Nobody else feels guilty.

ŚAKUNTALA. Your Majesty, pray forgive what we said when we did not know that you were present. I am afraid that we say a great many things behind a person's back.

KING (*smiling*).

> Your fault is pardoned if I may
>   Relieve my weariness
> By sitting on the flower-strewn couch
>   Your fevered members press.

PRIYAMVADA. But that will not be enough to satisfy him.

ŚAKUNTALA (*feigning anger*). Stop! You are a rude girl. You make fun of me when I am in this condition.

ANUSUYA (*looking out of the arbour*). Priyamvada, there is a little fawn, looking all about him. He has probably lost his mother and is trying to find her. I am going to help him.

PRIYAMVADA. He is a frisky little fellow. You can't catch him alone. I'll go with you. (*They start to go.*)

ŚAKUNTALA. I will not let you go and leave me alone.

THE TWO FRIENDS (*smiling*). You alone, when the king of the world is with you! (*Exeunt.*)

ŚAKUNTALA. Are my friends gone?

KING (*looking about*). Do not be anxious, beautiful Śakuntala. Have you not a humble servant here, to take the place of your friends? Then tell me:

> Shall I employ the moistened lotus-leaf
> To fan away your weariness and grief?
> Or take your lily feet upon my knee
> And rub them till you rest more easily?

ŚAKUNTALA. I will not offend against those to whom I owe honour. (*She rises weakly and starts to walk away.*)

KING (*detaining her*). The day is still hot, beautiful Śakuntala, and you are feverish.

> Leave not the blossom-dotted couch
> To wander in the midday heat,
> With lotus-petals on your breast,
> With fevered limbs and stumbling feet.

(*He lays his hand upon her.*)

ŚAKUNTALA. Oh, don't! Don't! For I am not mistress of myself. Yet what can I do now? I had no one to help me but my friends.

KING. I am rebuked.

ŚAKUNTALA. I was not thinking of your Majesty. I was accusing fate.

KING. Why accuse a fate that brings what you desire?

ŚAKUNTALA. Why not accuse a fate that robs me of self-control and tempts me with the virtues of another?

KING (*to himself*).

> Though deeply longing, maids are coy
> And bid their wooers wait;
> Though eager for united joy
> In love, they hesitate.

> Love cannot torture them, nor move
> Their hearts to sudden mating;
> Perhaps they even torture love
> By their procrastinating.

(ŚAKUNTALA *moves away.*)

KING.   Why should I not have my way? (*He approaches and seizes her dress.*)

ŚAKUNTALA.   Oh, sir! Be a gentleman. There are hermits wandering about.

KING.   Do not fear your family, beautiful Śakuntala. Father Kanva knows the holy law. He will not regret it.

> For many a hermit maiden who
> By simple, voluntary rite
> Dispensed with priest and witness, yet
> Found favour in her father's sight.

(*He looks about.*) Ah, I have come into the open air. (*He leaves* ŚAKUNTALA *and retraces his steps.*)

ŚAKUNTALA (*takes a step, then turns with an eager gesture*).   O King, I cannot do as you would have me. You hardly know me after this short talk. But oh, do not forget me.

KING.

> When evening comes, the shadow of the tree
> Is cast far forward, yet does not depart;
> Even so, belovèd, wheresoe'er you be,
> The thought of you can never leave my heart.

ŚAKUNTALA (*takes a few steps. To herself*).   Oh, oh! When I hear him speak so, my feet will not move away. I will hide in this amaranth hedge and see how long his love lasts. (*She hides and waits.*)

KING.   Oh, my belovèd, my love for you is my whole life, yet you leave me and go away without a thought.

> Your body, soft as siris-flowers,
> Engages passion's utmost powers;
> How comes it that your heart is hard
> As stalks that siris-blossoms guard?

ŚAKUNTALA.   When I hear this, I have no power to go.

KING.   What have I to do here, where she is not? (*He gazes on the ground.*) Ah, I cannot go.

> The perfumed lotus-chain
> That once was worn by her
> Fetters and keeps my heart
> A hopeless prisoner.

(*He lifts it reverently.*)

ŚAKUNTALA (*looking at her arm*).   Why, I was so weak and ill that when the lotus-bracelet fell off, I did not even notice it.

KING (*laying the lotus-bracelet on his heart*).   Ah!

> Once, dear, on your sweet arm it lay,
> And on my heart shall ever stay;
> Though you disdain to give me joy,
> I find it in a lifeless toy.

ŚAKUNTALA.   I cannot hold back after that. I will use the bracelet as an excuse for my coming. (*She approaches.*)

KING (*seeing her. Joyfully*).   The queen of my life! As soon as I complained, fate proved kind to me.

> No sooner did the thirsty bird
>   With parching throat complain,
> Than forming clouds in heaven stirred
>   And sent the streaming rain.

ŚAKUNTALA (*standing before the king*).   When I was going away, sir, I remembered that this lotus-bracelet had fallen from my arm, and I have come back for it. My heart seemed to tell me that you had taken it. Please give it back, or you will betray me, and yourself too, to the hermits.

KING.   I will restore it on one condition.

ŚAKUNTALA.   What condition?

KING.   That I may myself place it where it belongs.

ŚAKUNTALA (*to herself*).   What can I do? (*She approaches.*)

KING.   Let us sit on this stone bench. (*They walk to the bench and sit down.*)

KING (*taking* ŚAKUNTALA's *hand*).   Ah!

> When Shiva's anger burned the tree
>   Of love in quenchless fire,
> Did heavenly fate preserve a shoot
>   To deck my heart's desire?

ŚAKUNTALA (*feeling his touch*).   Hasten, my dear, hasten.

KING (*joyfully to himself*).   Now I am content. She speaks as a wife to her husband. (*Aloud.*) Beautiful Śakuntala, the clasp of the bracelet is not very firm. May I fasten it in another way?

ŚAKUNTALA (*smiling*).   If you like.

KING (*artfully delaying before he fastens it*).   See, my beautiful girl!

> The lotus-chain is dazzling white
> As is the slender moon at night.

Perhaps it was the moon on high
That joined her horns and left the sky,
Believing that your lovely arm
Would, more than heaven, enhance her charm.

ŚAKUNTALA. I cannot see it. The pollen from the lotus over my ear has blown into my eye.

KING (*smiling*). Will you permit me to blow it away?

ŚAKUNTALA. I should not like to be an object of pity. But why should I not trust you?

KING. Do not have such thoughts. A new servant does not transgress orders.

ŚAKUNTALA. It is this exaggerated courtesy that frightens me.

KING (*to himself*). I shall not break the bonds of this sweet servitude. (*He starts to raise her face to his.* ŚAKUNTALA *resists a little, then is passive.*)

KING. Oh, my bewitching girl, have no fear of me. (ŚAKUNTALA *darts a glance at him, then looks down. The king raises her face. Aside.*)

Her sweetly trembling lip
With virgin invitation
Provokes my soul to sip
Delighted fascination.

ŚAKUNTALA. You seem slow, dear, in fulfilling your promise.

KING. The lotus over your ear is so near your eye, and so like it, that I was confused. (*He gently blows her eye.*)

ŚAKUNTALA. Thank you. I can see quite well now. But I am ashamed not to make any return for your kindness.

KING. What more could I ask?

It ought to be enough for me
To hover round your fragrant face;
Is not the lotus-haunting bee
Content with perfume and with grace?

ŚAKUNTALA. But what does he do if he is not content?

KING. This! This! (*He draws her face to his.*)

A VOICE BEHIND THE SCENES. O sheldrake bride, bid your mate farewell. The night is come.

ŚAKUNTALA (*listening excitedly*). Oh, my dear, this is Mother Gautami, come to inquire about me. Please hide among the branches. (*The king conceals himself. Enter* GAUTAMI, *with a bowl in her hand.*)

GAUTAMI. Here is the holy water, my child. (*She sees* ŚAKUNTALA *and helps her to rise.*) So ill, and all alone here with the gods?

ŚAKUNTALA. It was just a moment ago that Priyamvada and Anusuya went down to the river.

GAUTAMI (*sprinkling* ŚAKUNTALA *with the holy water*). May you live long and happy, my child. Has the fever gone down? (*She touches her.*)

ŚAKUNTALA. There is a difference, mother.

GAUTAMI. The sun is setting. Come, let us go to the cottage.

ŚAKUNTALA (*weakly rising. To herself*). Oh, my heart, you delayed when your desire came of itself. Now see what you have done. (*She takes a step, then turns around. Aloud.*) O bower that took away my pain, I bid you farewell until another blissful hour.

(*Exeunt* ŚAKUNTALA *and* GAUTAMI.)

KING (*advancing with a sigh*). The path to happiness is strewn with obstacles.

> Her face, adorned with soft eye-lashes,
> Adorable with trembling flashes
> Of half-denial, in memory lingers;
> The sweet lips guarded by her fingers,
> The head that drooped upon her shoulder—
> Why was I not a little bolder?

Where shall I go now? Let me stay a moment in this bower where my belovèd lay. (*He looks about.*)

> The flower-strewn bed whereon her body tossed;
> The bracelet, fallen from her arm and lost;
> The dear love-missive, in the lotus-leaf
> Cut by her nails: assuage my absent grief
> And occupy my eyes—I have no power,
> Though she is gone, to leave the reedy bower.

(*He reflects.*) Alas! I did wrong to delay when I had found my love. So now

> If she will grant me but one other meeting,
> I'll not delay; for happiness is fleeting;
> So plans my foolish, self-defeated heart;
> But when she comes, I play the coward's part.

A VOICE BEHIND THE SCENES. O King!

> The flames rise heavenward from the evening altar;
>   And round the sacrifices, blazing high,
> Flesh-eating demons stalk, like red cloud-masses,
>   And cast colossal shadows on the sky.

KING (*listens. Resolutely*). Have no fear, hermits. I am here.

(*Exit.*)

ACT IV — ŚAKUNTALA'S DEPARTURE

SCENE I

(Enter the two friends, gathering flowers.)

ANUSUYA.   Priyamvada, dear Śakuntala has been properly married by the voluntary ceremony and she has a husband worthy of her. And yet I am not quite satisfied.

PRIYAMVADA.   Why not?

ANUSUYA.   The sacrifice is over and the good king was dismissed to-day by the hermits. He has gone back to the city and there he is surrounded by hundreds of court ladies. I wonder whether he will remember poor Śakuntala or not.

PRIYAMVADA.   You need not be anxious about that. Such handsome men are sure to be good. But there is something else to think about. I don't know what Father will have to say when he comes back from his pilgrimage and hears about it.

ANUSUYA.   I believe that he will be pleased.

PRIYAMVADA.   Why?

ANUSUYA.   Why not? You know he wanted to give his daughter to a lover worthy of her. If fate brings this about of itself, why shouldn't Father be happy?

PRIYAMVADA.   I suppose you are right. *(She looks at her flower-basket.)* My dear, we have gathered flowers enough for the sacrifice.

ANUSUYA.   But we must make an offering to the gods that watch over Śakuntala's marriage. We had better gather more.

PRIYAMVADA.   Very well. *(They do so.)*

A VOICE BEHIND THE SCENES.   Who will bid me welcome?

ANUSUYA *(listening)*.   My dear, it sounds like a guest announcing himself.

PRIYAMVADA.   Well, Śakuntala is near the cottage. *(Reflecting.)* Ah, but to-day her heart is far away. Come we must do with the flowers we have. *(They start to walk away.)*

THE VOICE.   Do you dare despise a guest like me?

> Because your heart, by loving fancies blinded,
>> Has scorned a guest in pious life grown old,
> Your lover shall forget you though reminded,
>> Or think of you as of a story told.

(The two girls listen and show dejection.)

PRIYAMVADA.   Oh, dear! The very thing has happened. The dear, absent-minded girl has offended some worthy man.

ANUSUYA (*looking ahead*).   My dear, this is no ordinary somebody. It is the great sage Durvasas, the irascible. See how he strides away!

PRIYAMVADA.   Nothing burns like fire. Run, fall at his feet, bring him back, while I am getting water to wash his feet.

ANUSUYA.   I will. (*Exit.*)

PRIYAMVADA (*stumbling*).   There! I stumbled in my excitement, and the flower-basket fell out of my hand. (*She collects the scattered flowers.* ANUSUYA *returns.*)

ANUSUYA.   My dear, he is anger incarnate. Who could appease him? But I softened him a little.

PRIYAMVADA.   Even that is a good deal for him. Tell me about it.

ANUSUYA.   When he would not turn back, I fell at his feet and prayed to him. "Holy sir," I said, "remember her former devotion and pardon this offence. Your daughter did not recognise your great and holy power to-day."

PRIYAMVADA.   And then——

ANUSUYA.   Then he said: "My words must be fulfilled. But the curse shall be lifted when her lover sees a gem which he has given her for a token." And so he vanished.

PRIYAMVADA.   We can breathe again. When the good king went away, he put a ring, engraved with his own name, on Śakuntala's finger to remember him by. That will save her.

ANUSUYA.   Come, we must finish the sacrifice for her. (*They walk about.*)

PRIYAMVADA (*gazing*).   Just look, Anusuya! There is the dear girl, with her cheek resting on her left hand. She looks like a painted picture. She is thinking about him. How could she notice a guest when she has forgotten herself?

ANUSUYA.   Priyamvada, we two must keep this thing to ourselves. We must be careful of the dear girl. You know how delicate she is.

PRIYAMVADA.   Would any one sprinkle a jasmine-vine with scalding water?

(Exeunt ambo.)

SCENE II—Early Morning

(Enter a pupil of KANVA, *just risen from sleep.)*

PUPIL.   Father Kanva has returned from his pilgrimage, and has bidden me find out what time it is. I will go into the open air and see how much of the night remains. (*He walks and looks about.*) See! The dawn is breaking. For already

> The moon behind the western mount is sinking;
>   The eastern sun is heralded by dawn;
> From heaven's twin lights, their fall and glory linking,
>   Brave lessons of submission may be drawn.

And again:

> Night-blooming lilies, when the moon is hidden,
>   Have naught but memories of beauty left.
> Hard, hard to bear! Her lot whom heaven has bidden
>   To live alone, of love and lover reft.

And again:

> On jujube-trees the blushing dewdrops falter;
>   The peacock wakes and leaves the cottage thatch;
> A deer is rising near the hoof-marked altar,
>   And stretching, stands, the day's new life to catch.

And yet again:

> The moon that topped the loftiest mountain ranges,
>   That slew the darkness in the midmost sky,
> Is fallen from heaven, and all her glory changes:
>   So high to rise, so low at last to lie!

ANUSUYA (*entering hurriedly. To herself*).   That is just what happens to the innocent. Sakuntala has been treated shamefully by the king.

PUPIL.   I will tell Father Kanva that the hour of morning sacrifice is come. (*Exit.*)

ANUSUYA.   The dawn is breaking. I am awake bright and early. But what shall I do now that I am awake? My hands refuse to attend to the ordinary morning tasks. Well, let love take its course. For the dear, pure-minded girl trusted him—the traitor! Perhaps it is not the good king's fault. It must be the curse of Durvasas. Otherwise, how could the good king say such beautiful things, and then let all this time pass without even sending a message? (*She reflects.*) Yes, we must send him the ring he left as a token. But whom shall we ask to take it? The hermits are unsympathetic because they have never suffered. It seemed as if her friends were to blame and so, try as we might, we could not tell Father Kanva that Śakuntala was married to Dushyanta and was expecting a baby. Oh, what shall we do? (*Enter* PRIYAMVADA.)

PRIYAMVADA.   Hurry, Anusuya, hurry! We are getting Śakuntala ready for her journey.

ANUSUYA (*astonished*).   What do you mean, my dear?

PRIYAMVADA.   Listen. I just went to Śakuntala, to ask if she had slept well.

ANUSUYA.   And then——

PRIYAMVADA.   I found her hiding her face for shame, and Father Kanva was embracing her and encouraging her. "My child," he said, "I bring you joy. The offering fell straight in the sacred fire, and auspicious smoke rose toward the sacrificer. My pains for you have proved like instruction given to a good student; they have brought me no regret. This very day I shall give you an escort of hermits and send you to your husband."

ANUSUYA.   But, my dear, who told Father Kanva about it?

PRIYAMVADA.   A voice from heaven that recited a verse when he had entered the fire-sanctuary.

ANUSUYA (*astonished*).   What did it say?

PRIYAMVADA.   Listen. (*Speaking in good Sanskrit.*)

> Know, Brahman, that your child,
>   Like the fire-pregnant tree,
> Bears kingly seed that shall be born
>   For earth's prosperity.

ANUSUYA (*hugging* PRIYAMVADA).   I am so glad, dear. But my joy is half sorrow when I think that Śakuntala is going to be taken away this very day.

PRIYAMVADA.   We must hide our sorrow as best we can. The poor girl must be made happy to-day.

ANUSUYA.   Well, here is a cocoa-nut casket, hanging on a branch of the mango-tree. I put flower-pollen in it for this very purpose. It keeps fresh, you know. Now you wrap it in a lotus-leaf, and I will get yellow pigment and earth from a sacred spot and blades of panic grass for the happy ceremony. (PRIYAMVADA *does so. Exit* ANUSUYA.)

A VOICE BEHIND THE SCENES.   Gautami, bid the worthy Sharngarava and Sharadvata make ready to escort my daughter Śakuntala.

PRIYAMVADA (*listening*).   Hurry, Anusuya, hurry! They are calling the hermits who are going to Hastinapura. (*Enter* ANUSUYA, *with materials for the ceremony.*)

ANUSUYA.   Come, dear, let us go. (*They walk about.*)

PRIYAMVADA (*looking ahead*).   There is Śakuntala. She took the ceremonial bath at sunrise, and now the hermit-women are giving her rice-cakes and wishing her happiness. Let's go to her. (*They do so. Enter* ŚAKUNTALA *with attendants as described, and* GAUTAMI.)

ŚAKUNTALA.   Holy women, I salute you.

GAUTAMI.   My child, may you receive the happy title "queen," showing that your husband honours you.

HERMIT-WOMEN.   My dear, may you become the mother of a hero. (*Exeunt all but* GAUTAMI.)

THE TWO FRIENDS (*approaching*).   Did you have a good bath, dear?

ŚAKUNTALA.   Good morning, girls. Sit here.

THE TWO FRIENDS (*seating themselves*).   Now stand straight, while we go through the happy ceremony.

ŚAKUNTALA.   It has happened often enough, but I ought to be very grateful to-day. Shall I ever be adorned by my friends again? (*She weeps.*)

THE TWO FRIENDS.   You ought not to weep, dear, at this happy time. (*They wipe the tears away and adorn her.*)

PRIYAMVADA.   You are so beautiful, you ought to have the finest gems. It seems like an insult to give you these hermitage things. (*Enter* HARITA, *a hermit-youth, with ornaments.*)

HARITA.   Here are ornaments for our lady. (*The women look at them in astonishment.*)

GAUTAMI.   Harita, my son, whence come these things?

HARITA.   From the holy power of Father Kanva.

GAUTAMI.   A creation of his mind?

HARITA.   Not quite. Listen. Father Kanva sent us to gather blossoms from the trees for Śakuntala, and then

> One tree bore fruit, a silken marriage dress
> That shamed the moon in its white loveliness;
> Another gave us lac-dye for the feet;
> From others, fairy hands extended, sweet
> Like flowering twigs, as far as to the wrist,
> And gave us gems, to adorn her as we list.

PRIYAMVADA (*looking at* ŚAKUNTALA).   A bee may be born in a hole in a tree, but she likes the honey of the lotus.

GAUTAMI.   This gracious favour is a token of the queenly happiness which you are to enjoy in your husband's palace. (ŚAKUNTALA *shows embarrassment.*)

HARITA.   Father Kanva has gone to the bank of the Malini, to perform his ablutions. I will tell him of the favour shown us by the trees. (*Exit.*)

ANUSUYA.   My dear, we poor girls never saw such ornaments. How

shall we adorn you? (*She stops to think, and to look at the ornaments.*)
But we have seen pictures. Perhaps we can arrange them right.

ŚAKUNTALA.   I know how clever you are. (*The two friends adorn her.
Enter* KANVA, *returning after his ablutions.*)

KANVA.

> Śakuntala must go to-day;
>   I miss her now at heart;
> I dare not speak a loving word
>   Or choking tears will start.
>
> My eyes are dim with anxious thought;
>   Love strikes me to the life:
> And yet I strove for pious peace—
>   I have no child, no wife.
>
> What must a father feel, when come
> The pangs of parting from his child at home?

(*He walks about.*)

THE TWO FRIENDS.   There, Śakuntala, we have arranged your ornaments. Now put on this beautiful silk dress. (ŚAKUNTALA *rises and does
so.*)

GAUTAMI.   My child, here is your father. The eyes with which he
seems to embrace you are overflowing with tears of joy. You must greet
him properly. (ŚAKUNTALA *makes a shamefaced reverence.*)

KANVA.   My child,

> Like Sharmishtha, Yayati's wife,
>   Win favour measured by your worth;
> And may you bear a kingly son
>   Like Puru, who shall rule the earth.

GAUTAMI.   My child, this is not a prayer, but a benediction.

KANVA.   My daughter, walk from left to right about the fires in
which the offering has just been thrown. (*All walk about.*)

> The holy fires around the altar kindle,
>   And at their margins sacred grass is piled;
> Beneath their sacrificial odours dwindle
>   Misfortunes. May the fires protect you, child!

(ŚAKUNTALA *walks about them from left to right.*)

KANVA.   Now you may start, my daughter. (*He glances about.*)
Where are Sharngarava and Sharadvata? (*Enter the two pupils.*)

THE TWO PUPILS.   We are here, Father.

KANVA.   Sharngarava, my son, lead the way for your sister.

SHARNGARAVA.   Follow me. (*They all walk about.*)

KANVA.   O trees of the pious grove, in which the fairies dwell,

> She would not drink till she had wet
>   Your roots, a sister's duty,
> Nor pluck your flowers; she loves you yet
>   Far more than selfish beauty.
>
> 'Twas festival in her pure life
>   When budding blossoms showed;
> And now she leaves you as a wife—
>   Oh, speed her on her road!

SHARNGARAVA (*listening to the song of koïl-birds*).   Father,

> The trees are answering your prayer
>   In cooing cuckoo-song,
> Bidding Sakuntala farewell,
>   Their sister for so long.

INVISIBLE BEINGS.

> May lily-dotted lakes delight your eye;
>   May shade-trees bid the heat of noonday cease;
> May soft winds blow the lotus-pollen nigh;
>   May all your path be pleasantness and peace.

(All listen in astonishment.)

GAUTAMI.   My child, the fairies of the pious grove bid you farewell. For they love the household. Pay reverence to the holy ones.

SAKUNTALA (*does so. Aside to* PRIYAMVADA).   Priyamvada, I long to see my husband, and yet my feet will hardly move. It is hard, hard to leave the hermitage.

PRIYAMVADA.   You are not the only one to feel sad at this farewell. See how the whole grove feels at parting from you.

> The grass drops from the feeding doe;
>   The peahen stops her dance;
> Pale, trembling leaves are falling slow,
>   The tears of clinging plants.

SAKUNTALA (*recalling something*).   Father, I must say good-bye to the spring-creeper, my sister among the vines.

KANVA.   I know your love for her. See! Here she is at your right hand.

SAKUNTALA (*approaches the vine and embraces it*).   Vine sister, embrace me too with your arms, these branches. I shall be far away from you after to-day. Father, you must care for her as you did for me.

KANVA.　　　　My child, you found the lover who
　　　　　　　　Had long been sought by me;
　　　　　　　No longer need I watch for you;
　　　　　　　I'll give the vine a lover true,
　　　　　　　　This handsome mango-tree.

And now start on your journey.

ŚAKUNTALA (*going to the two friends*).　Dear girls, I leave her in your care too.

THE TWO FRIENDS.　But who will care for poor us? (*They shed tears.*)

KANVA.　Anusuya! Priyamvada! Do not weep. It is you who should cheer Śakuntala. (*All walk about.*)

ŚAKUNTALA.　Father, there is the pregnant doe, wandering about near the cottage. When she becomes a happy mother, you must send some one to bring me the good news. Do not forget.

KANVA.　I shall not forget, my child.

ŚAKUNTALA (*stumbling*).　Oh, oh! Who is it that keeps pulling at my dress, as if to hinder me? (*She turns round to see.*)

KANVA.

　　　　　　　It is the fawn whose lip, when torn
　　　　　　　　By kusha-grass, you soothed with oil;
　　　　　　　The fawn who gladly nibbled corn
　　　　　　　　Held in your hand; with loving toil
　　　　　　　You have adopted him, and he
　　　　　　　Would never leave you willingly.

ŚAKUNTALA.　My dear, why should you follow me when I am going away from home? Your mother died when you were born and I brought you up. Now I am leaving you, and Father Kanva will take care of you. Go back, dear! Go back! (*She walks away, weeping.*)

KANVA.　Do not weep, my child. Be brave. Look at the path before you.

　　　　　　　Be brave, and check the rising tears
　　　　　　　　That dim your lovely eyes;
　　　　　　　Your feet are stumbling on the path
　　　　　　　　That so uneven lies.

SHARNGARAVA.　Holy Father, the Scripture declares that one should accompany a departing loved one only to the first water. Pray give us your commands on the bank of this pond, and then return.

KANVA.　Then let us rest in the shade of this fig-tree. (*All do so.*) What commands would it be fitting for me to lay on King Dushyanta? (*He reflects.*)

ANUSUYA.　My dear, there is not a living thing in the whole hermitage that is not grieving to-day at saying good-bye to you. Look!

> The sheldrake does not heed his mate
> Who calls behind the lotus-leaf;
> He drops the lily from his bill
> And turns on you a glance of grief.

KANVA. Son Sharngarava, when you present Śakuntala to the king, give him this message from me.

> Remembering my religious worth,
> Your own high race, the love poured forth
> By her, forgetful of her friends,
> Pay her what honour custom lends
> To all your wives. And what fate gives
> Beyond, will please her relatives.

SHARNGARAVA. I will not forget your message, Father.

KANVA (*turning to* ŚAKUNTALA). My child, I must now give you my counsel. Though I live in the forest, I have some knowledge of the world.

SHARNGARAVA. True wisdom, Father, gives insight into everything.

KANVA. My child, when you have entered your husband's home,

> Obey your elders; and be very kind
> To rivals; never be perversely blind
> And angry with your husband, even though he
> Should prove less faithful than a man might be;
> Be as courteous to servants as you may,
> Not puffed with pride in this your happy day:
> Thus does a maiden grow into a wife;
> But self-willed women are the curse of life.

But what does Gautami say?

GAUTAMI. This is advice sufficient for a bride. (*To* ŚAKUNTALA.) You will not forget, my child.

KANVA. Come, my daughter, embrace me and your friends.

ŚAKUNTALA. Oh, Father! Must my friends turn back too?

KANVA. My daughter, they too must some day be given in marriage. Therefore they may not go to court. Gautami will go with you.

ŚAKUNTALA (*throwing her arms about her father*). I am torn from my father's breast like a vine stripped from a sandal-tree on the Malabar hills. How can I live in another soil? (*She weeps.*)

KANVA. My daughter, why distress yourself so?

> A noble husband's honourable wife,
> You are to spend a busy, useful life
> In the world's eye; and soon, as eastern skies

Bring forth the sun, from you there shall arise
A child, a blessing and a comfort strong—
You will not miss me, dearest daughter, long.

ŚAKUNTALA (*falling at his feet*).   Farewell, Father.

KANVA.   My daughter, may all that come to you which I desire for you.

ŚAKUNTALA (*going to her two friends*).   Come, girls! Embrace me, both of you together.

THE TWO FRIENDS (*do so*).   Dear, if the good king should perhaps be slow to recognise you, show him the ring with his own name engraved on it.

ŚAKUNTALA.   Your doubts make my heart beat faster.

THE TWO FRIENDS.   Do not be afraid, dear. Love is timid.

SHARNGARAVA (*looking about*).   Father, the sun is in mid-heaven. She must hasten.

ŚAKUNTALA (*embracing* KANVA *once more*).   Father, when shall I see the pious grove again?

KANVA.   My daughter,

> When you have shared for many years
>   The king's thoughts with the earth,
> When to a son who knows no fears
>   You shall have given birth,
>
> When, trusted to the son you love,
>   Your royal labours cease,
> Come with your husband to the grove
>   And end your days in peace.

GAUTAMI.   My child, the hour of your departure is slipping by. Bid your father turn back. No, she would never do that. Pray turn back, sir.

KANVA.   Child, you interrupt my duties in the pious grove.

ŚAKUNTALA.   Yes, Father. You will be busy in the grove. You will not miss me. But oh! I miss you.

KANVA.   How can you think me so indifferent? (*He sighs.*)

> My lonely sorrow will not go,
>   For seeds you scattered here
> Before the cottage door, will grow;
>   And I shall see them, dear.

Go. And peace go with you. (*Exit* ŚAKUNTALA, *with* GAUTAMI, SHARNGARAVA, *and* SHARADVATA.)

THE TWO FRIENDS (*gazing long after her. Mournfully*).   Oh, oh! Śakuntala is lost among the trees.

KANVA. Anusuya! Priyamvada! Your companion is gone. Choke down your grief and follow me. (*They start to go back.*)

THE TWO FRIENDS. Father, the grove seems empty without Śakuntala.

KANVA. So love interprets. (*He walks about, sunk in thought.*) Ah! I have sent Śakuntala away, and now I am myself again. For

> A girl is held in trust, another's treasure;
> To arms of love my child to-day is given;
> And now I feel a calm and sacred pleasure;
> I have restored the pledge that came from heaven.

(*Exeunt omnes.*)

ACT V — ŚAKUNTALA'S REJECTION

(Enter a chamberlain.)

CHAMBERLAIN *(sighing)*. Alas! To what a state am I reduced!

> I once assumed the staff of reed
> For custom's sake alone,
> As officer to guard at need
> The ladies round the throne.
> But years have passed away and made
> It serve, my tottering steps to aid.

The king is within. I will tell him of the urgent business which demands his attention. *(He takes a few steps.)* But what is the business? *(He recalls it.)* Yes, I remember. Certain hermits, pupils of Kanva, desire to see his Majesty. Strange, strange!

> The mind of age is like a lamp
> Whose oil is running thin;
> One moment it is shining bright,
> Then darkness closes in.

(He walks and looks about.) Here is his Majesty.

> He does not seek — until a father's care
> Is shown his subjects — rest in solitude;
> As a great elephant recks not of the sun
> Until his herd is sheltered in the wood.

In truth, I hesitate to announce the coming of Kanva's pupils to the king. For he has this moment risen from the throne of justice. But kings are never weary. For

> The sun unyokes his horses never;
> Blows night and day the breeze;
> Shesha upholds the world forever:
> And kings are like to these.

45

(*He walks about. Enter the king, the clown, and retinue according to rank.*)

KING (*betraying the cares of office*).   Every one is happy on attaining his desire—except a king. His difficulties increase with his power. Thus:

> Security slays nothing but ambition;
> With great possessions, troubles gather thick;
> Pain grows, not lessens, with a king's position,
> As when one's hand must hold the sunshade's stick.

TWO COURT POETS BEHIND THE SCENES.   Victory to your Majesty.
FIRST POET.

> The world you daily guard and bless,
> Not heeding pain or weariness;
>   Thus is your nature made.
> A tree will brave the noonday, when
> The sun is fierce, that weary men
>   May rest beneath its shade.

SECOND POET.

> Vice bows before the royal rod;
> Strife ceases at your kingly nod;
>   You are our strong defender.
> Friends come to all whose wealth is sure,
> But you, alike to rich and poor,
>   Are friend both strong and tender.

KING (*listening*).   Strange! I was wearied by the demands of my office, but this renews my spirit.

CLOWN.   Does a bull forget that he is tired when you call him the leader of the herd?

KING (*smiling*).   Well, let us sit down. (*They seat themselves, and the retinue arranges itself. A lute is heard behind the scenes.*)

CLOWN (*listening*).   My friend, listen to what is going on in the music-room. Some one is playing a lute, and keeping good time. I suppose Lady Hansavati is practising.

KING.   Be quiet. I wish to listen.

CHAMBERLAIN (*looks at the king*).   Ah, the king is occupied. I must await his leisure. (*He stands aside.*)

A SONG BEHIND THE SCENES.

> You who kissed the mango-flower,
>   Honey-loving bee,
> Gave her all your passion's power,
>   Ah, so tenderly!

> How can you be tempted so
>   By the lily, pet?
> Fresher honey 's sweet, I know;
>   But can you forget?

KING.   What an entrancing song!

CLOWN.   But, man, don't you understand what the words mean?

KING (*smiling*).   I was once devoted to Queen Hansavati. And the rebuke comes from her. Friend Madhavya, tell Queen Hansavati in my name that the rebuke is a very pretty one.

CLOWN.   Yes, sir. (*He rises.*) But, man, you are using another fellow's fingers to grab a bear's tail-feathers with. I have about as much chance of salvation as a monk who hasn't forgotten his passions.

KING.   Go. Soothe her like a gentleman.

CLOWN.   I suppose I must. (*Exit.*)

KING (*to himself*).   Why am I filled with wistfulness on hearing such a song? I am not separated from one I love. And yet

> In face of sweet presentment
>   Or harmonies of sound,
> Man e'er forgets contentment,
>   By wistful longings bound.

> There must be recollections
>   Of things not seen on earth,
> Deep nature's predilections,
>   Loves earlier than birth.

(*He shows the wistfulness that comes from unremembered things.*)

CHAMBERLAIN (*approaching*).   Victory to your Majesty. Here are hermits who dwell in the forest at the foot of the Himalayas. They bring women with them, and they carry a message from Kanva. What is your pleasure with regard to them?

KING (*astonished*).   Hermits? Accompanied by women? From Kanva?

CHAMBERLAIN.   Yes.

KING.   Request my chaplain Somarata in my name to receive these hermits in the manner prescribed by Scripture, and to conduct them himself before me. I will await them in a place fit for their reception.

CHAMBERLAIN.   Yes, your Majesty. (*Exit.*)

KING (*rising*).   Vetravati, conduct me to the fire-sanctuary.

PORTRESS.   Follow me, your Majesty. (*She walks about.*) Your Majesty, here is the terrace of the fire-sanctuary. It is beautiful, for it has just been swept, and near at hand is the cow that yields the milk of sacrifice. Pray ascend it.

KING (*ascends and stands leaning on the shoulder of an attendant*). Vetravati, with what purpose does Father Kanva send these hermits to me?

> Do leaguèd powers of sin conspire
> To balk religion's pure desire?
> Has wrong been done to beasts that roam
> Contented round the hermits' home?
> Do plants no longer bud and flower,
> To warn me of abuse of power?
> These doubts and more assail my mind,
> But leave me puzzled, lost, and blind.

PORTRESS. How could these things be in a hermitage that rests in the fame of the king's arm? No, I imagine they have come to pay homage to their king, and to congratulate him on his pious role.
(*Enter the chaplain and the chamberlain, conducting the two pupils of* KANVA, *with* GAUTAMI *and* ŚAKUNTALA.)
CHAMBERLAIN. Follow me, if you please.
SHARNGARAVA. Friend Sharadvata,

> The king is noble and to virtue true;
>   None dwelling here commit the deed of shame;
> Yet we ascetics view the worldly crew
>   As in a house all lapped about with flame.

SHARADVATA. Sharngarava, your emotion on entering the city is quite just. As for me,

> Free from the world and all its ways,
> I see them spending worldly days
> As clean men view men smeared with oil,
> As pure men, those whom passions soil,
> As waking men view men asleep,
> As free men, those in bondage deep.

CHAPLAIN. That is why men like you are great.
ŚAKUNTALA (*observing an evil omen*). Oh, why does my right eye throb?
GAUTAMI. Heaven avert the omen, my child. May happiness wait upon you. (*They walk about.*)
CHAPLAIN (*indicating the king*). O hermits, here is he who protects those of every station and of every age. He has already risen, and awaits you. Behold him.
SHARNGARAVA. Yes, it is admirable, but not surprising. For

Fruit-laden trees bend down to earth;
  The water-pregnant clouds hang low;
Good men are not puffed up by power—
  The unselfish are by nature so.

PORTRESS.   Your Majesty, the hermits seem to be happy. They give
you gracious looks.
KING (*observing* ŚAKUNTALA).   Ah!

Who is she, shrouded in the veil
  That dims her beauty's lustre,
Among the hermits like a flower
  Round which the dead leaves cluster?

PORTRESS.   Your Majesty, she is well worth looking at.
KING.   Enough! I must not gaze upon another's wife.
ŚAKUNTALA (*laying her hand on her breast. Aside*).   Oh, my heart,
why tremble so? Remember his constant love and be brave.
CHAPLAIN (*advancing*).   Hail, your Majesty. The hermits have been
received as Scripture enjoins. They have a message from their teacher.
May you be pleased to hear it.
KING (*respectfully*).   I am all attention.
THE TWO PUPILS (*raising their right hands*).   Victory, O King.
KING (*bowing low*).   I salute you all.
THE TWO PUPILS.   All hail.
KING.   Does your pious life proceed without disturbance?
THE TWO PUPILS.

How could the pious duties fail
  While you defend the right?
Or how could darkness' power prevail
  O'er sunbeams shining bright?

KING (*to himself*).   Indeed, my royal title is no empty one. (*Aloud.*)
Is holy Kanva in health?
SHARNGARAVA.   O King, those who have religious power can com-
mand health. He asks after your welfare and sends this message.
KING.   What are his commands?
SHARNGARAVA.   He says: "Since you have met this my daughter and
have married her, I give you my glad consent. For

You are the best of worthy men, they say;
  And she, I know, Good Works personified;
The Creator wrought for ever and a day,
  In wedding such a virtuous groom and bride.

She is with child. Take her and live with her in virtue."

GAUTAMI. Bless you, sir. I should like to say that no one invites me to speak.

KING. Speak, mother.

GAUTAMI.

> Did she with father speak or mother?
> Did you engage her friends in speech?
> Your faith was plighted each to other;
> Let each be faithful now to each.

ŚAKUNTALA. What will my husband say?

KING (*listening with anxious suspicion*). What is this insinuation?

ŚAKUNTALA (*to herself*). Oh, oh! So haughty and so slanderous!

SHARNGARAVA. "What is this insinuation?" What is your question? Surely you know the world's ways well enough.

> Because the world suspects a wife
>   Who does not share her husband's lot,
> Her kinsmen wish her to abide
>   With him, although he love her not.

KING. You cannot mean that this young woman is my wife.

ŚAKUNTALA (*sadly to herself*). Oh, my heart, you feared it, and now it has come.

SHARNGARAVA. O King,

> A king, and shrink when love is done,
>   Turn coward's back on truth, and flee!

KING. What means this dreadful accusation?

SHARNGARAVA (*furiously*).

> O drunk with power! We might have known
>   That you were steeped in treachery.

KING. A stinging rebuke!

GAUTAMI (*to* ŚAKUNTALA). Forget your shame, my child. I will remove your veil. Then your husband will recognise you. (*She does so.*)

KING (*observing* ŚAKUNTALA. *To himself*).

> As my heart ponders whether I could ever
>   Have wed this woman that has come to me
> In tortured loveliness, as I endeavour
>   To bring it back to mind, then like a bee

> That hovers round a jasmine flower at dawn,
>   While frosty dews of morning still o'erweave it,
> And hesitates to sip ere they be gone,
>   I cannot taste the sweet, and cannot leave it.

PORTRESS (*to herself*).   What a virtuous king he is! Would any other man hesitate when he saw such a pearl of a woman coming of her own accord?

SHARNGARAVA.   Have you nothing to say, O King?

KING.   Hermit, I have taken thought. I cannot believe that this woman is my wife. She is plainly with child. How can I take her, confessing myself an adulterer?

ŚAKUNTALA (*to herself*).   Oh, oh, oh! He even casts doubt on our marriage. The vine of my hope climbed high, but it is broken now.

SHARNGARAVA.   Not so.

> You scorn the sage who rendered whole
>   His child befouled, and choked his grief,
> Who freely gave you what you stole
>   And added honour to a thief!

SHARADVATA.   Enough, Sharngarava. Śakuntala, we have said what we were sent to say. You hear his words. Answer him.

ŚAKUNTALA (*to herself*).   He loved me so. He is so changed. Why remind him? Ah, but I must clear my own character. Well, I will try. (*Aloud.*) My dear husband— (*She stops.*) No, he doubts my right to call him that. Your Majesty, it was pure love that opened my poor heart to you in the hermitage. Then you were kind to me and gave me your promise. Is it right for you to speak so now, and to reject me?

KING (*stopping his ears*).   Peace, peace!

> A stream that eats away the bank,
>   Grows foul, and undermines the tree.
> So you would stain your honour, while
>   You plunge me into misery.

ŚAKUNTALA.   Very well. If you have acted so because you really fear to touch another man's wife, I will remove your doubts with a token you gave me.

KING.   An excellent idea!

ŚAKUNTALA (*touching her finger*).   Oh, oh! The ring is lost. (*She looks sadly at* GAUTAMI.)

GAUTAMI.   My child, you worshipped the holy Ganges at the spot where Indra descended. The ring must have fallen there.

KING.   Ready wit, ready wit!

ŚAKUNTALA.   Fate is too strong for me there. I will tell you something else.

KING.   Let me hear what you have to say.

ŚAKUNTALA.   One day, in the bower of reeds, you were holding a lotus-leaf cup full of water.

KING. I hear you.

ŚAKUNTALA. At that moment the fawn came up, my adopted son. Then you took pity on him and coaxed him. "Let him drink first," you said. But he did not know you, and he would not come to drink water from your hand. But he liked it afterwards, when I held the very same water. Then you smiled and said: "It is true. Every one trusts his own sort. You both belong to the forest."

KING. It is just such women, selfish, sweet, false, that entice fools.

GAUTAMI. You have no right to say that. She grew up in the pious grove. She does not know how to deceive.

KING. Old hermit woman,

> The female's untaught cunning may be seen
> In beasts, far more in women selfish-wise;
> The cuckoo's eggs are left to hatch and rear
> By foster-parents, and away she flies.

ŚAKUNTALA (*angrily*). Wretch! You judge all this by your own false heart. Would any other man do what you have done? To hide behind virtue, like a yawning well covered over with grass!

KING (*to himself*). But her anger is free from coquetry, because she has lived in the forest. See!

> Her glance is straight; her eyes are flashing red;
> Her speech is harsh, not drawlingly well-bred;
> Her whole lip quivers, seems to shake with cold;
> Her frown has straightened eyebrows arching bold.

No, she saw that I was doubtful, and her anger was feigned. Thus

> When I refused but now
>   Hard-heartedly, to know
> Of love or secret vow,
>   Her eyes grew red; and so,
> Bending her arching brow,
>   She fiercely snapped Love's bow.

(*Aloud.*) My good girl, Dushyanta's conduct is known to the whole kingdom, but not this action.

ŚAKUNTALA. Well, well. I had my way. I trusted a king, and put myself in his hands. He had a honey face and a heart of stone. (*She covers her face with her dress and weeps.*)

SHARNGARAVA. Thus does unbridled levity burn.

> Be slow to love, but yet more slow
>   With secret mate;

With those whose hearts we do not know,
  Love turns to hate.

KING.   Why do you trust this girl, and accuse me of an imaginary
crime?

SHARNGARAVA (*disdainfully*).   You have learned your wisdom upside
down.

It would be monstrous to believe
  A girl who never lies;
Trust those who study to deceive
  And think it very wise.

KING.   Aha, my candid friend! Suppose I were to admit that I am
such a man. What would happen if I deceived the girl?

SHARNGARAVA.   Ruin.

KING.   It is unthinkable that ruin should fall on Puru's line.

SHARNGARAVA.   Why bandy words? We have fulfilled our Father's
bidding. We are ready to return.

Leave her or take her, as you will;
  She is your wife;
Husbands have power for good or ill
  O'er woman's life.

Gautami, lead the way. (*They start to go.*)

ŚAKUNTALA.   He has deceived me shamelessly. And will you leave
me too? (*She starts to follow.*)

GAUTAMI (*turns around and sees her*).   Sharngarava, my son, Śakuntala is following us, lamenting piteously. What can the poor child do
with a husband base enough to reject her?

SHARNGARAVA (*turns angrily*).   You self-willed girl! Do you dare
show independence? (ŚAKUNTALA *shrinks in fear*.) Listen.

If you deserve such scorn and blame,
What will your father with your shame?
But if you know your vows are pure,
Obey your husband and endure.

Remain. We must go.

KING.   Hermit, why deceive this woman? Remember:

Night-blossoms open to the moon,
  Day-blossoms to the sun;
A man of honour ever strives
  Another's wife to shun.

SHARNGARAVA.   O King, suppose you had forgotten your former actions in the midst of distractions. Should you now desert your wife — you who fear to fail in virtue?

KING.   I ask *you* which is the heavier sin:

> Not knowing whether I be mad
> Or falsehood be in her,
> Shall I desert a faithful wife
> Or turn adulterer?

CHAPLAIN (*considering*).   Now if this were done——

KING.   Instruct me, my teacher.

CHAPLAIN.   Let the woman remain in my house until her child is born.

KING.   Why this?

CHAPLAIN.   The chief astrologers have told you that your first child was destined to be an emperor. If the son of the hermit's daughter is born with the imperial birthmarks, then welcome her and introduce her into the palace. Otherwise, she must return to her father.

KING.   It is good advice, my teacher.

CHAPLAIN (*rising*).   Follow me, my daughter.

ŚAKUNTALA.   O mother earth, give me a grave! (*Exit weeping, with the chaplain, the hermits, and* GAUTAMI. *The king, his memory clouded by the curse, ponders on* ŚAKUNTALA.)

VOICES BEHIND THE SCENES.   A miracle! A miracle!

KING (*listening*).   What does this mean? (*Enter the chaplain.*)

CHAPLAIN (*in amazement*).   Your Majesty, a wonderful thing has happened.

KING.   What?

CHAPLAIN.   When Kanva's pupils had departed,

> She tossed her arms, bemoaned her plight,
> Accused her crushing fate——

KING.   What then?

CHAPLAIN.

> Before our eyes a heavenly light
> In woman's form, but shining bright,
> Seized her and vanished straight.

(*All betray astonishment.*)

KING.   My teacher, we have already settled the matter. Why speculate in vain? Let us seek repose.

CHAPLAIN.   Victory to your Majesty. (*Exit.*)

KING.   Vetravati, I am bewildered. Conduct me to my apartment.

PORTRESS.   Follow me, your Majesty.
KING (*walks about. To himself*).

>   With a hermit-wife I had no part,
>   All memories evade me;
>   And yet my sad and stricken heart
>   Would more than half persuade me.

(*Exeunt omnes.*)

ACT VI — SEPARATION FROM ŚAKUNTALA

SCENE I — In the street before the Palace

*(Enter the chief of police, two policemen,
and a man with his hands bound behind his back.)*

THE TWO POLICEMEN (*striking the man*).   Now, pickpocket, tell us where you found this ring. It is the king's ring, with letters engraved on it, and it has a magnificent great gem.

FISHERMAN (*showing fright*).   Be merciful, kind gentlemen. I am not guilty of such a crime.

FIRST POLICEMAN.   No, I suppose the king thought you were a pious Brahman, and made you a present of it.

FISHERMAN.   Listen, please. I am a fisherman, and I live on the Ganges, at the spot where Indra came down.

SECOND POLICEMAN.   You thief, we didn't ask for your address or your social position.

CHIEF.   Let him tell a straight story, Suchaka. Don't interrupt.

THE TWO POLICEMEN.   Yes, chief. Talk, man, talk.

FISHERMAN.   I support my family with things you catch fish with— nets, you know, and hooks, and things.

CHIEF (*laughing*).   You have a sweet trade.

FISHERMAN.   Don't say that, master.

> You can't give up a lowdown trade
>   That your ancestors began;
> A butcher butchers things, and yet
>   He's the tenderest-hearted man.

CHIEF.   Go on. Go on.

FISHERMAN.   Well, one day I was cutting up a carp. In its maw I saw this ring with the magnificent great gem. And then I was just trying to sell it here when you kind gentlemen grabbed me. That is the only way I got it. Now kill me, or find fault with me.

CHIEF (*smelling the ring*).   There is no doubt about it, Januka. It has been in a fish's maw. It has the real perfume of raw meat. Now we have to find out how he got it. We must go to the palace.

THE TWO POLICEMEN (*to the fisherman*). Move on, you cutpurse, move on. (*They walk about.*)

CHIEF. Suchaka, wait here at the big gate until I come out of the palace. And don't get careless.

THE TWO POLICEMEN. Go in, chief. I hope the king will be nice to you.

CHIEF. Good-bye. (*Exit.*)

SUCHAKA. Januka, the chief is taking his time.

JANUKA. You can't just drop in on a king.

SUCHAKA. Januka, my fingers are itching (*indicating the fisherman*) to kill this cutpurse.

FISHERMAN. Don't kill a man without any reason, master.

JANUKA (*looking ahead*). There is the chief, with a written order from the king. (*To the fisherman.*) Now you will see your family, or else you will feed the crows and jackals. (*Enter the chief.*)

CHIEF. Quick! Quick! (*He breaks off.*)

FISHERMAN. Oh, oh! I'm a dead man. (*He shows dejection.*)

CHIEF. Release him, you. Release the fishnet fellow. It is all right, his getting the ring. Our king told me so himself.

SUCHAKA. All right, chief. He is a dead man come back to life. (*He releases the fisherman.*)

FISHERMAN (*bowing low to the chief*). Master, I owe you my life. (*He falls at his feet.*)

CHIEF. Get up, get up! Here is a reward that the king was kind enough to give you. It is worth as much as the ring. Take it. (*He hands the fisherman a bracelet.*)

FISHERMAN (*joyfully taking it*). Much obliged.

JANUKA. He *is* much obliged to the king. Just as if he had been taken from the stake and put on an elephant's back.

SUCHAKA. Chief, the reward shows that the king thought a lot of the ring. The gem must be worth something.

CHIEF. No, it wasn't the fine gem that pleased the king. It was this way.

THE TWO POLICEMEN. Well?

CHIEF. I think, when the king saw it, he remembered somebody he loves. You know how dignified he is usually. But as soon as he saw it, he broke down for a moment.

SUCHAKA. You have done the king a good turn, chief.

JANUKA. All for the sake of this fish-killer, it seems to me. (*He looks enviously at the fisherman.*)

FISHERMAN. Take half of it, masters, to pay for something to drink.

JANUKA.   Fisherman, you are the biggest and best friend I've got. The first thing we want, is all the brandy we can hold. Let's go where they keep it.   (*Exeunt omnes.*)

SCENE II — In the Palace Gardens

(*Enter* MISHRAKESHI, *flying through the air.*)

MISHRAKESHI.   I have taken my turn in waiting upon the nymphs. And now I will see what this good king is doing. Sakuntala is like a second self to me, because she is the daughter of Menaka. And it was she who asked me to do this. (*She looks about.*) It is the day of the spring festival. But I see no preparations for a celebration at court. I might learn the reason by my power of divination. But I must do as my friend asked me. Good! I will make myself invisible and stand near these girls who take care of the garden. I shall find out that way. (*She descends to earth. Enter a maid, gazing at a mango branch, and behind her, a second.*)

FIRST MAID.

> First mango-twig, so pink, so green,
>   First living breath of spring,
> You are sacrificed as soon as seen,
>   A festival offering.

SECOND MAID.   What are you chirping about to yourself, little cuckoo?

FIRST MAID.   Why, little bee, you know that the cuckoo goes crazy with delight when she sees the mango-blossom.

SECOND MAID (*joyfully*).   Oh, has the spring really come?

FIRST MAID.   Yes, little bee. And this is the time when you too buzz about in crazy joy.

SECOND MAID.   Hold me, dear, while I stand on tiptoe and offer this blossom to Love, the divine.

FIRST MAID.   If I do, you must give me half the reward of the offering.

SECOND MAID.   That goes without saying, dear. We two are one. (*She leans on her friend and takes the mango-blossom.*) Oh, see! The mango-blossom hasn't opened, but it has broken the sheath, so it is fragrant. (*She brings her hands together.*) I worship mighty Love.

> O mango-twig I give to Love
>   As arrow for his bow,
> Most sovereign of his arrows five,
>   Strike maiden-targets low.

(*She throws the twig. Enter the chamberlain.*)

CHAMBERLAIN (*angrily*).   Stop, silly girl. The king has strictly forbidden the spring festival. Do you dare pluck the mango-blossoms?

THE TWO MAIDS (*frightened*).   Forgive us, sir. We did not know.

CHAMBERLAIN.   What! You have not heard the king's command, which is obeyed even by the trees of spring and the creatures that dwell in them. See!

> The mango branches are in bloom,
>   Yet pollen does not form;
> The cuckoo's song sticks in his throat,
>   Although the days are warm;
>
> The amaranth-bud is formed, and yet
>   Its power of growth is gone;
> The love-god timidly puts by
>   The arrow he has drawn.

MISHRAKESHI.   There is no doubt of it. This good king has wonderful power.

FIRST MAID.   A few days ago, sir, we were sent to his Majesty by his brother-in-law Mitravasu to decorate the garden. That is why we have heard nothing of this affair.

CHAMBERLAIN.   You must not do so again.

THE TWO MAIDS.   But we are curious. If we girls may know about it, pray tell us, sir. Why did his Majesty forbid the spring festival?

MISHRAKESHI.   Kings are fond of celebrations. There must be some good reason.

CHAMBERLAIN (*to himself*).   It is in everybody's mouth. Why should I not tell it? (*Aloud.*) Have you heard the gossip concerning Śakuntala's rejection?

THE TWO MAIDS.   Yes, sir. The king's brother-in-law told us, up to the point where the ring was recovered.

CHAMBERLAIN.   There is little more to tell. When his Majesty saw the ring, he remembered that he had indeed contracted a secret marriage with Śakuntala, and had rejected her under a delusion. And then he fell a prey to remorse.

> He hates the things he loved; he intermits
> The daily audience, nor in judgment sits;
> Spends sleepless nights in tossing on his bed;
> At times, when he by courtesy is led
> To address a lady, speaks another name,
> Then stands for minutes, sunk in helpless shame.

MISHRAKESHI.   I am glad to hear it.

CHAMBERLAIN.   His Majesty's sorrow has forbidden the festival.

THE TWO MAIDS.   It is only right.

A VOICE BEHIND THE SCENES.   Follow me.

CHAMBERLAIN (*listening*).   Ah, his Majesty approaches. Go, and attend to your duties. (*Exeunt the two maids. Enter the king, wearing a dress indicative of remorse; the clown, and the portress.*)

CHAMBERLAIN (*observing the king*).   A beautiful figure charms in whatever state. Thus, his Majesty is pleasing even in his sorrow. For

> All ornament is laid aside; he wears
> One golden bracelet on his wasted arm;
> His lip is scorched by sighs; and sleepless cares
> Redden his eyes. Yet all can work no harm
> On that magnificent beauty, wasting, but
> Gaining in brilliance, like a diamond cut.

MISHRAKESHI (*observing the king*).   No wonder Sakuntala pines for him, even though he dishonoured her by his rejection of her.

KING (*walks about slowly, sunk in thought*).

> Alas! My smitten heart, that once lay sleeping,
> Heard in its dreams my fawn-eyed love's laments,
> And wakened now, awakens but to weeping,
> To bitter grief, and tears of penitence.

MISHRAKESHI.   That is the poor girl's fate.

CLOWN (*to himself*).   He has got his Sakuntala-sickness again. I wish I knew how to cure him.

CHAMBERLAIN (*advancing*).   Victory to your Majesty. I have examined the garden. Your Majesty may visit its retreats.

KING.   Vetravati, tell the minister Pishuna in my name that a sleepless night prevents me from mounting the throne of judgment. He is to investigate the citizens' business and send me a memorandum.

PORTRESS.   Yes, your Majesty. (*Exit.*)

KING.   And you, Parvatayana, return to your post of duty.

CHAMBERLAIN.   Yes, your Majesty. (*Exit.*)

CLOWN.   You have got rid of the vermin. Now amuse yourself in this garden. It is delightful with the passing of the cold weather.

KING (*sighing*).   My friend, the proverb makes no mistake. Misfortune finds the weak spot. See!

> No sooner did the darkness lift
> That clouded memory's power,
> Than the god of love prepared his bow
> And shot the mango-flower.

No sooner did the ring recall
My banished maiden dear,
No sooner do I vainly weep
For her, than spring is here.

CLOWN. Wait a minute, man. I will destroy Love's arrow with my stick. (*He raises his stick and strikes at the mango branch.*)

KING (*smiling*). Enough! I see your pious power. My friend, where shall I sit now to comfort my eyes with the vines? They remind me somehow of her.

CLOWN. Well, you told one of the maids, the clever painter, that you would spend this hour in the bower of spring-creepers. And you asked her to bring you there the picture of the lady Śakuntala which you painted on a tablet.

KING. It is my only consolation. Lead the way to the bower of spring-creepers.

CLOWN. Follow me. (*They walk about.* MISHRAKESHI *follows.*) Here is the bower of spring-creepers, with its jewelled benches. Its loneliness seems to bid you a silent welcome. Let us go in and sit down. (*They do so.*)

MISHRAKESHI. I will hide among the vines and see the dear girl's picture. Then I shall be able to tell her how deep her husband's love is. (*She hides.*)

KING (*sighing*). I remember it all now, my friend. I told you how I first met Śakuntala. It is true, you were not with me when I rejected her. But I had told you of her at the first. Had you forgotten, as I did?

MISHRAKESHI. This shows that a king should not be separated a single moment from some intimate friend.

CLOWN. No, I didn't forget. But when you had told the whole story, you said it was a joke and there was nothing in it. And I was fool enough to believe you. No, this is the work of fate.

MISHRAKESHI. It must be.

KING (*after meditating a moment*). Help me, my friend.

CLOWN. But, man, this isn't right at all. A good man never lets grief get the upper hand. The mountains are calm even in a tempest.

KING. My friend, I am quite forlorn. I keep thinking of her pitiful state when I rejected her. Thus:

When I denied her, then she tried
To join her people. "Stay," one cried,
Her father's representative.
She stopped, she turned, she could but give
A tear-dimmed glance to heartless me—
That arrow burns me poisonously.

MISHRAKESHI. How his fault distresses him!

CLOWN. Well, I don't doubt it was some heavenly being that carried her away.

KING. Who else would dare to touch a faithful wife? Her friends told me that Menaka was her mother. My heart persuades me that it was she, or companions of hers, who carried Śakuntala away.

MISHRAKESHI. His madness was wonderful, not his awakening reason.

CLOWN. But in that case, you ought to take heart. You will meet her again.

KING. How so?

CLOWN. Why, a mother or a father cannot long bear to see a daughter separated from her husband.

KING. My friend,

> And was it phantom, madness, dream,
>   Or fatal retribution stern?
> My hopes fell down a precipice
>   And never, never will return.

CLOWN. Don't talk that way. Why, the ring shows that incredible meetings do happen.

KING (*looking at the ring*). This ring deserves pity. It has fallen from a heaven hard to earn.

> Your virtue, ring, like mine,
>   Is proved to be but small;
> Her pink-nailed finger sweet
>   You clasped. How could you fall?

MISHRAKESHI. If it were worn on any other hand, it would deserve pity. My dear girl, you are far away. I am the only one to hear these delightful words.

CLOWN. Tell me how you put the ring on her finger.

MISHRAKESHI. He speaks as if prompted by my curiosity.

KING. Listen, my friend. When I left the pious grove for the city, my darling wept and said: "But how long will you remember us, dear?"

CLOWN. And then you said——

KING. Then I put this engraved ring on her finger, and said to her——

CLOWN. Well, what?

KING.

> Count every day one letter of my name;
>   Before you reach the end, dear,

> Will come to lead you to my palace halls
> A guide whom I shall send, dear.

Then, through my madness, it fell out cruelly.

MISHRAKESHI.   It was too charming an agreement to be frustrated by fate.

CLOWN.   But how did it get into a carp's mouth, as if it had been a fish-hook?

KING.   While she was worshipping the Ganges at Shachitirtha, it fell.

CLOWN.   I see.

MISHRAKESHI.   That is why the virtuous king doubted his marriage with poor Śakuntala. Yet such love does not ask for a token. How could it have been?

KING.   Well, I can only reproach this ring.

CLOWN (*smiling*).   And I will reproach this stick of mine. Why are you crooked when I am straight?

KING (*not hearing him*).

> How could you fail to linger
> On her soft, tapering finger,
>   And in the water fall?

And yet

> Things lifeless know not beauty;
> But I—I scorned my duty,
>   The sweetest task of all.

MISHRAKESHI.   He has given the answer which I had ready.

CLOWN.   But that is no reason why I should starve to death.

KING (*not heeding*).   O my darling, my heart burns with repentance because I abandoned you without reason. Take pity on me. Let me see you again. (*Enter a maid with a tablet.*)

MAID.   Your Majesty, here is the picture of our lady. (*She produces the tablet.*)

KING (*gazing at it*).   It is a beautiful picture. See!

> A graceful arch of brows above great eyes;
> Lips bathed in darting, smiling light that flies
> Reflected from white teeth; a mouth as red
> As red karkandhu-fruit; love's brightness shed
> O'er all her face in bursts of liquid charm—
> The picture speaks, with living beauty warm.

CLOWN (*looking at it*).   The sketch is full of sweet meaning. My eyes seem to stumble over its uneven surface. What more can I say? I expect to see it come to life, and I feel like speaking to it.

MISHRAKESHI.   The king is a clever painter. I seem to see the dear girl before me.

KING.   My friend,

> What in the picture is not fair,
>   Is badly done;
> Yet something of her beauty there,
>   I feel, is won.

MISHRAKESHI.   This is natural, when love is increased by remorse.

KING (*sighing*).

> I treated her with scorn and loathing ever;
>   Now o'er her pictured charms my heart will burst:
> A traveller I, who scorned the mighty river,
>   And seeks in the mirage to quench his thirst.

CLOWN.   There are three figures in the picture, and they are all beautiful. Which one is the lady Śakuntala?

MISHRAKESHI.   The poor fellow never saw her beauty. His eyes are useless, for she never came before them.

KING.   Which one do you think?

CLOWN (*observing closely*).   I think it is this one, leaning against the creeper which she has just sprinkled. Her face is hot and the flowers are dropping from her hair; for the ribbon is loosened. Her arms droop like weary branches; she has loosened her girdle, and she seems a little fatigued. This, I think, is the lady Śakuntala, the others are her friends.

KING.   You are good at guessing. Besides, here are proofs of my love.

> See where discolorations faint
>   Of loving handling tell;
> And here the swelling of the paint
>   Shows where my sad tears fell.

Chaturika, I have not finished the background. Go, get the brushes.

MAID.   Please hold the picture, Madhavya, while I am gone.

KING.   I will hold it. (*He does so. Exit maid.*)

CLOWN.   What are you going to add?

MISHRAKESHI.   Surely, every spot that the dear girl loved.

KING.   Listen, my friend.

> The stream of Malini, and on its sands
> The swan-pairs resting; holy foot-hill lands
> Of great Himalaya's sacred ranges, where

> The yaks are seen; and under trees that bear
> Bark hermit-dresses on their branches high,
> A doe that on the buck's horn rubs her eye.

CLOWN (*aside*).   To hear him talk, I should think he was going to fill up the picture with heavy-bearded hermits.

KING.   And another ornament that Śakuntala loved I have forgotten to paint.

CLOWN.   What?

MISHRAKESHI.   Something natural for a girl living in the forest.

KING.

> The siris-blossom, fastened o'er her ear,
>   Whose stamens brush her cheek;
> The lotus-chain like autumn moonlight soft
>   Upon her bosom meek.

CLOWN.   But why does she cover her face with fingers lovely as the pink water-lily? She seems frightened. (*He looks more closely.*) I see. Here is a bold, bad bee. He steals honey, and so he flies to her lotus-face.

KING.   Drive him away.

CLOWN.   It is your affair to punish evil-doers.

KING.   True. O welcome guest of the flowering vine, why do you waste your time in buzzing here?

> Your faithful, loving queen,
>   Perched on a flower, athirst,
> Is waiting for you still,
>   Nor tastes the honey first.

MISHRAKESHI.   A gentlemanly way to drive him off!

CLOWN.   This kind are obstinate, even when you warn them.

KING (*angrily*).   Will you not obey my command? Then listen:

> 'Tis sweet as virgin blossoms on a tree,
> The lip I kissed in love-feasts tenderly;
> Sting that dear lip, O bee, with cruel power,
> And you shall be imprisoned in a flower.

CLOWN.   Well, he doesn't seem afraid of your dreadful punishment. (*Laughing. To himself.*) The man is crazy, and I am just as bad, from associating with him.

KING.   Will he not go, though I warn him?

MISHRAKESHI.   Love works a curious change even in a brave man.

CLOWN (*aloud*).   It is only a picture, man.

KING.   A picture?

MISHRAKESHI.   I too understand it now. But to him, thoughts are real experiences.

KING.   You have done an ill-natured thing.

> When I was happy in the sight,
>   And when my heart was warm,
> You brought sad memories back, and made
>   My love a painted form.   (*He sheds a tear.*)

MISHRAKESHI.   Fate plays strangely with him.

KING.   My friend, how can I endure a grief that has no respite?

> I cannot sleep at night
>   And meet her dreaming;
> I cannot see the sketch
>   While tears are streaming.

MISHRAKESHI.   My friend, you have indeed atoned—and in her friend's presence—for the pain you caused by rejecting dear Śakuntala. (*Enter the maid* CHATURIKA.)

MAID.   Your Majesty, I was coming back with the box of paint-brushes——

KING.   Well?

MAID.   I met Queen Vasumati with the maid Pingalika. And the queen snatched the box from me, saying: "I will take it to the king myself."

CLOWN.   How did you escape?

MAID.   The queen's dress caught on a vine. And while her maid was setting her free, I excused myself in a hurry.

A VOICE BEHIND THE SCENES.   Follow me, your Majesty.

CLOWN (*listening*).   Man, the she-tiger of the palace is making a spring on her prey. She means to make one mouthful of the maid.

KING.   My friend, the queen has come because she feels touched in her honour. You had better take care of this picture.

CLOWN.   "And yourself," you might add. (*He takes the picture and rises.*) If you get out of the trap alive, call for me at the Cloud Balcony. And I will hide the thing there so that nothing but a pigeon could find it.   (*Exit on the run.*)

MISHRAKESHI.   Though his heart is given to another, he is courteous to his early flame. He is a constant friend. (*Enter the portress with a document.*)

PORTRESS.   Victory to your Majesty.

KING.   Vetravati, did you not meet Queen Vasumati?

PORTRESS.   Yes, your Majesty. But she turned back when she saw that I carried a document.

KING.   The queen knows times and seasons. She will not interrupt business.

PORTRESS.   Your Majesty, the minister sends word that in the press of various business he has attended to only one citizen's suit. This he has reduced to writing for your Majesty's perusal.

KING.   Give me the document. (*The portress does so.*)

KING (*reads*).   "Be it known to his Majesty. A seafaring merchant named Dhanavriddhi has been lost in a shipwreck. He is childless, and his property, amounting to several millions, reverts to the crown. Will his Majesty take action?" (*Sadly.*) It is dreadful to be childless. Vetravati, he had great riches. There must be several wives. Let inquiry be made. There may be a wife who is with child.

PORTRESS.   We have this moment heard that a merchant's daughter of Saketa is his wife. And she is soon to become a mother.

KING.   The child shall receive the inheritance. Go, inform the minister.

PORTRESS.   Yes, your Majesty. (*She starts to go.*)

KING.   Wait a moment.

PORTRESS (*turning back*).   Yes, your Majesty.

KING.   After all, what does it matter whether he have issue or not?

> Let King Dushyanta be proclaimed
>   To every sad soul kin
> That mourns a kinsman loved and lost,
>   Yet did not plunge in sin.

PORTRESS.   The proclamation shall be made. (*She goes out and soon returns.*) Your Majesty, the royal proclamation was welcomed by the populace as is a timely shower.

KING (*sighing deeply*).   Thus, when issue fails, wealth passes, on the death of the head of the family, to a stranger. When I die, it will be so with the glory of Puru's line.

PORTRESS.   Heaven avert the omen!

KING.   Alas! I despised the happiness that offered itself to me.

MISHRAKESHI.   Without doubt, he has dear Śakuntala in mind when he thus reproaches himself.

KING.

> Could I forsake the virtuous wife
> Who held my best, my future life
> And cherished it for glorious birth,
> As does the seed-receiving earth?

MISHRAKESHI.   She will not long be forsaken.

MAID (*to the portress*).   Mistress, the minister's report has doubled our lord's remorse. Go to the Cloud Balcony and bring Madhavya to dispel his grief.

PORTRESS. A good suggestion. (*Exit.*)

KING. Alas! The ancestors of Dushyanta are in a doubtful case.

> For I am childless, and they do not know,
>   When I am gone, what child of theirs will bring
> The scriptural oblation; and their tears
>   Already mingle with my offering.

MISHRAKESHI. He is screened from the light, and is in darkness.

MAID. Do not give way to grief, your Majesty. You are in the prime of your years, and the birth of a son to one of your other wives will make you blameless before your ancestors. (*To herself.*) He does not heed me. The proper medicine is needed for any disease.

KING (*betraying his sorrow*). Surely,

> The royal line that flowed
>   A river pure and grand,
> Dies in the childless king,
>   Like streams in desert sand. (*He swoons.*)

MAID (*in distress*). Oh, sir, come to yourself.

MISHRAKESHI. Shall I make him happy now? No, I heard the mother of the gods consoling Śakuntala. She said that the gods, impatient for the sacrifice, would soon cause him to welcome his true wife. I must delay no longer. I will comfort dear Śakuntala with my tidings. (*Exit through the air.*)

A VOICE BEHIND THE SCENES. Help, help!

KING (*comes to himself and listens*). It sounds as if Madhavya were in distress.

MAID. Your Majesty, I hope that Pingalika and the other maids did not catch poor Madhavya with the picture in his hands.

KING. Go, Chaturika. Reprove the queen in my name for not controlling her servants.

MAID. Yes, your Majesty. (*Exit.*)

THE VOICE. Help, help!

KING. The Brahman's voice seems really changed by fear. Who waits without? (*Enter the chamberlain.*)

CHAMBERLAIN. Your Majesty commands?

KING. See why poor Madhavya is screaming so.

CHAMBERLAIN. I will see. (*He goes out, and returns trembling.*)

KING. Parvatayana, I hope it is nothing very dreadful.

CHAMBERLAIN. I hope not.

KING. Then why do you tremble so? For

> Why should the trembling, born
> Of age, increasing, seize
> Your limbs and bid them shake
> Like fig-leaves in the breeze?

CHAMBERLAIN.   Save your friend, O King!

KING.   From what?

CHAMBERLAIN.   From great danger.

KING.   Speak plainly, man.

CHAMBERLAIN.   On the Cloud Balcony, open to the four winds of heaven——

KING.   What has happened there?

CHAMBERLAIN.

> While he was resting on its height,
> Which palace peacocks in their flight
> Can hardly reach, he seemed to be
> Snatched up—by what, we could not see.

KING (*rising quickly*).   My very palace is invaded by evil creatures. To be a king, is to be a disappointed man.

> The moral stumblings of mine own,
> The daily slips, are scarcely known;
> Who then that rules a kingdom, can
> Guide every deed of every man?

THE VOICE.   Hurry, hurry!

KING (*hears the voice and quickens his steps*).   Have no fear, my friend.

THE VOICE.   Have no fear! When something has got me by the back of the neck, and is trying to break my bones like a piece of sugar-cane!

KING (*looks about*).   A bow! a bow! (*Enter a Greek woman with a bow.*)

GREEK WOMAN.   A bow and arrows, your Majesty. And here are the finger-guards. (*The king takes the bow and arrows.*)

ANOTHER VOICE BEHIND THE SCENES.

> Writhe, while I drink the red blood flowing clear
> And kill you, as a tiger kills a deer;
> Let King Dushyanta grasp his bow; but how
> Can all his kingly valour save you now?

KING (*angrily*).   He scorns me, too! In one moment, miserable demon, you shall die. (*Stringing his bow.*) Where is the stairway, Parvatayana?

CHAMBERLAIN.   Here, your Majesty. (*All make haste.*)

KING (*looking about*).   There is no one here.

THE CLOWN'S VOICE.   Save me, save me! I see you, if you can't see me. I am a mouse in the claws of the cat. I am done for.

KING.   You are proud of your invisibility. But shall not my arrow see you? Stand still. Do not hope to escape by clinging to my friend.

> My arrow, flying when the bow is bent,
> Shall slay the wretch and spare the innocent;
> When milk is mixed with water in a cup,
> Swans leave the water, and the milk drink up.

> (*He takes aim. Enter* MATALI *and the clown*.)

MATALI.   O King, as Indra, king of the gods, commands,

> Seek foes among the evil powers alone;
>   For them your bow should bend;
> Not cruel shafts, but glances soft and kind
>   Should fall upon a friend.

KING (*hastily withdrawing the arrow*).   It is Matali. Welcome to the charioteer of heaven's king.

CLOWN.   Well! He came within an inch of butchering me. And you welcome him.

MATALI (*smiling*).   Hear, O King, for what purpose Indra sends me to you.

KING.   I am all attention.

MATALI.   There is a host of demons who call themselves Invincible—the brood of Kalanemi.

KING.   So Narada has told me.

MATALI.

> Heaven's king is powerless; you shall smite
>   His foes in battle soon;
> Darkness that overcomes the day,
>   Is scattered by the moon.

Take your bow at once, enter my heavenly chariot, and set forth for victory.

KING.   I am grateful for the honour which Indra shows me. But why did you act thus toward Madhavya?

MATALI.   I will tell you. I saw that you were overpowered by some inner sorrow, and acted thus to rouse you. For

> The spurnèd snake will swell his hood;
>   Fire blazes when 'tis stirred;
> Brave men are roused to fighting mood
>   By some insulting word.

KING. Friend Madhavya, I must obey the bidding of heaven's king. Go, acquaint the minister Pishuna with the matter, and add these words of mine:

> Your wisdom only shall control
> The kingdom for a time;
> My bow is strung; a distant goal
> Calls me, and tasks sublime.

CLOWN. Very well. (*Exit.*)

MATALI. Enter the chariot. (*The king does so. Exeunt omnes.*)

ACT VII

(Enter, in a chariot that flies through the air, the king and MATALI.*)*

KING.   Matali, though I have done what Indra commanded, I think myself an unprofitable servant, when I remember his most gracious welcome.

MATALI.   O King, know that each considers himself the other's debtor. For

> You count the service given
>> Small by the welcome paid,
> Which to the king of heaven
>> Seems mean for such brave aid.

KING.   Ah, no! For the honour given me at parting went far beyond imagination. Before the gods, he seated me beside him on his throne. And then

> He smiled, because his son Jayanta's heart
>> Beat quicker, by the self-same wish oppressed,
> And placed about my neck the heavenly wreath
>> Still fragrant from the sandal on his breast.

MATALI.   But what do you not deserve from heaven's king? Remember:

> Twice, from peace-loving Indra's sway
> The demon-thorn was plucked away:
>> First, by Man-lion's crooked claws;
> Again, by your smooth shafts to-day.

KING.   This merely proves Indra's majesty. Remember:

> All servants owe success in enterprise
>> To honour paid before the great deed's done;
> Could dawn defeat the darkness otherwise
>> Than resting on the chariot of the sun?

MATALI. The feeling becomes you. (*After a little.*) See, O King! Your glory has the happiness of being published abroad in heaven.

> With colours used by nymphs of heaven
>   To make their beauty shine,
> Gods write upon the surface given
>   Of many a magic vine,
> As worth their song, the simple story
> Of those brave deeds that made your glory.

KING. Matali, when I passed before, I was intent on fighting the demons, and did not observe this region. Tell me. In which path of the winds are we?
MATALI.

> It is the windpath sanctified
> By holy Vishnu's second stride;
> Which, freed from dust of passion, ever
> Upholds the threefold heavenly river;
> And, driving them with reins of light,
> Guides the stars in wheeling flight.

KING. That is why serenity pervades me, body and soul. (*He observes the path taken by the chariot.*) It seems that we have descended into the region of the clouds.
MATALI. How do you perceive it?
KING.

> Plovers that fly from mountain-caves,
> Steeds that quick-flashing lightning laves,
> And chariot-wheels that drip with spray—
> A path o'er pregnant clouds betray.

MATALI. You are right. And in a moment you will be in the world over which you bear rule.
KING (*looking down*). Matali, our quick descent gives the world of men a mysterious look. For

> The plains appear to melt and fall
> From mountain peaks that grow more tall;
> The trunks of trees no longer hide
> Nor in their leafy nests abide;
> The river network now is clear,
> For smaller streams at last appear:
> It seems as if some being threw
> The world to me, for clearer view.

MATALI. You are a good observer, O King. (*He looks down, awe-struck.*) There is a noble loveliness in the earth.

KING. Matali, what mountain is this, its flanks sinking into the eastern and into the western sea? It drips liquid gold like a cloud at sunset.

MATALI. O King, this is Gold Peak, the mountain of the fairy centaurs. Here it is that ascetics most fully attain to magic powers. See!

> The ancient sage, Marichi's son,
> Child of the Uncreated One,
> Father of superhuman life,
> Dwells here austerely with his wife.

KING (*reverently*). I must not neglect the happy chance. I cannot go farther until I have walked humbly about the holy one.

MATALI. It is a worthy thought, O King. (*The chariot descends.*) We have come down to earth.

KING (*astonished*). Matali,

> The wheels are mute on whirling rim;
> Unstirred, the dust is lying there;
> We do not bump the earth, but skim:
> Still, still we seem to fly through air.

MATALI. Such is the glory of the chariot which obeys you and Indra.

KING. In which direction lies the hermitage of Marichi's son?

MATALI (*pointing*). See!

> Where stands the hermit, horridly austere,
> Whom clinging vines are choking, tough and sere;
> Half-buried in an ant-hill that has grown
> About him, standing post-like and alone;
> Sun-staring with dim eyes that know no rest,
> The dead skin of a serpent on his breast:
> So long he stood unmoved, insensate there
> That birds build nests within his mat of hair.

KING (*gazing*). All honour to one who mortifies the flesh so terribly.

MATALI (*checking the chariot*). We have entered the hermitage of the ancient sage, whose wife Aditi tends the coral-trees.

KING. Here is deeper contentment than in heaven. I seem plunged in a pool of nectar.

MATALI (*stopping the chariot*). Descend, O King.

KING (*descending*). But how will you fare?

MATALI. The chariot obeys the word of command. I too will

descend. (*He does so.*) Before you, O King, are the groves where the holiest hermits lead their self-denying life.

KING.   I look with amazement both at their simplicity and at what they might enjoy.

> Their appetites are fed with air
> Where grows whatever is most fair;
> They bathe religiously in pools
> Which golden lily-pollen cools;
> They pray within a jewelled home,
> Are chaste where nymphs of heaven roam:
> They mortify desire and sin
> With things that others fast to win.

MATALI.   The desires of the great aspire high. (*He walks about and speaks to some one not visible.*) Ancient Shakalya, how is Marichi's holy son occupied? (*He listens.*) What do you say? That he is explaining to Aditi, in answer to her question, the duties of a faithful wife? My matter must await a fitter time. (*He turns to the king.*) Wait here, O King, in the shade of the ashoka tree, till I have announced your coming to the sire of Indra.

KING.   Very well. (*Exit* MATALI. *The king's arm throbs, a happy omen.*)

> I dare not hope for what I pray;
>   Why thrill—in vain?
> For heavenly bliss once thrown away
>   Turns into pain.

A VOICE BEHIND THE SCENES.   Don't! You mustn't be so foolhardy. Oh, you are always the same.

KING (*listening*).   No naughtiness could feel at home in this spot. Who draws such a rebuke upon himself? (*He looks towards the sound. In surprise.*) It is a child, but no child in strength. And two hermit-women are trying to control him.

> He drags a struggling lion cub,
>   The lioness' milk half-sucked, half-missed,
> Towzles his mane, and tries to drub
>   Him tame with small, imperious fist.

(*Enter a small boy, as described, and two hermit-women.*)

BOY.   Open your mouth, cub. I want to count your teeth.

FIRST WOMAN.   Naughty boy, why do you torment our pets? They are like children to us. Your energy seems to take the form of striking something. No wonder the hermits call you All-tamer.

KING.   Why should my heart go out to this boy as if he were my own son? (*He reflects.*) No doubt my childless state makes me sentimental.

SECOND WOMAN.   The lioness will spring at you if you don't let her baby go.

BOY (*smiling*).   Oh, I'm dreadfully scared. (*He bites his lip.*)

KING (*in surprise*).

> The boy is seed of fire
>   Which, when it grows, will burn;
> A tiny spark that soon
>   To awful flame may turn.

FIRST WOMAN.   Let the little lion go, dear. I will give you another plaything.

BOY.   Where is it? Give it to me. (*He stretches out his hand.*)

KING (*looking at the hand*).   He has one of the imperial birthmarks! For

> Between the eager fingers grow
>   The close-knit webs together drawn,
> Like some lone lily openings slow
>   To meet the kindling blush of dawn.

SECOND WOMAN.   Suvrata, we can't make him stop by talking. Go. In my cottage you will find a painted clay peacock that belongs to the hermit-boy Mankanaka. Bring him that.

FIRST WOMAN.   I will. (*Exit.*)

BOY.   Meanwhile I'll play with this one.

HERMIT-WOMAN (*looks and laughs*).   Let him go.

KING.   My heart goes out to this wilful child. (*Sighing.*)

> They show their little buds of teeth
>   In peals of causeless laughter;
> They hide their trustful heads beneath
>   Your heart. And stumbling after
> Come sweet, unmeaning sounds that sing
>   To you. The father warms
> And loves the very dirt they bring
>   Upon their little forms.

HERMIT-WOMAN (*shaking her finger*).   Won't you mind me? (*She looks about.*) Which one of the hermit-boys is here? (*She sees the king.*) Oh, sir, please come here and free this lion cub. The little rascal is tormenting him, and I can't make him let go.

KING.   Very well. (*He approaches, smiling.*) O little son of a great sage!

Your conduct in this place apart,
    Is most unfit;
'Twould grieve your father's pious heart
    And trouble it.

To animals he is as good
    As good can be;
You spoil it, like a black snake's brood
    In sandal tree.

HERMIT-WOMAN.   But, sir, he is not the son of a hermit.
KING.   So it would seem, both from his looks and his actions. But in this spot, I had no suspicion of anything else. (*He loosens the boy's hold on the cub, and touching him, says to himself.*)

It makes me thrill to touch the boy,
    The stranger's son, to me unknown;
What measureless content must fill
    The man who calls the child his own!

HERMIT-WOMAN (*looking at the two*).   Wonderful! wonderful!
KING.   Why do you say that, mother?
HERMIT-WOMAN.   I am astonished to see how much the boy looks like you, sir. You are not related. Besides, he is a perverse little creature and he does not know you. Yet he takes no dislike to you.
KING (*caressing the boy*).   Mother, if he is not the son of a hermit, what is his family?
HERMIT-WOMAN.   The family of Puru.
KING (*to himself*).   He is of one family with me! Then could my thought be true? (*Aloud.*) But this is the custom of Puru's line:

In glittering palaces they dwell
While men, and rule the country well;
Then make the grove their home in age,
And die in austere hermitage.

But how could human beings, of their own mere motion, attain this spot?
HERMIT-WOMAN.   You are quite right, sir. But the boy's mother was related to a nymph, and she bore her son in the pious grove of the father of the gods.
KING (*to himself*).   Ah, a second ground for hope. (*Aloud.*) What was the name of the good king whose wife she was?
HERMIT-WOMAN.   Who would speak his name? He rejected his true wife.
KING (*to himself*).   This story points at me. Suppose I ask the boy for

his mother's name. (*He reflects.*) No, it is wrong to concern myself with one who may be another's wife. (*Enter the first woman, with the clay peacock.*)

FIRST WOMAN.   Look, All-tamer. Here is the bird, the *śakunta*. Isn't the *śakunta* lovely?

BOY (*looks about*).   Where is my mamma? (*The two women burst out laughing.*)

FIRST WOMAN.   It sounded like her name, and deceived him. He loves his mother.

SECOND WOMAN.   She said: "See how pretty the peacock is." That is all.

KING (*to himself*).   His mother's name is Śakuntala! But names are alike. I trust this hope may not prove a disappointment in the end, like a mirage.

BOY.   I like this little peacock, sister. Can it fly? (*He seizes the toy.*)

FIRST WOMAN (*looks at the boy. Anxiously*).   Oh, the amulet is not on his wrist.

KING.   Do not be anxious, mother. It fell while he was struggling with the lion cub. (*He starts to pick it up.*)

THE TWO WOMEN.   Oh, don't, don't! (*They look at him.*) He has touched it! (*Astonished, they lay their hands on their bosoms, and look at each other.*)

KING.   Why did you try to prevent me?

FIRST WOMAN.   Listen, your Majesty. This is a divine and most potent charm, called the Invincible. Marichi's holy son gave it to the baby when the birth-ceremony was performed. If it falls on the ground, no one may touch it except the boy's parents or the boy himself.

KING.   And if another touch it?

FIRST WOMAN.   It becomes a serpent and stings him.

KING.   Did you ever see this happen to any one else?

BOTH WOMEN.   More than once.

KING (*joyfully*).   Then why may I not welcome my hopes fulfilled at last? (*He embraces the boy.*)

SECOND WOMAN.   Come, Suvrata. Śakuntala is busy with her religious duties. We must go and tell her what has happened. (*Exeunt ambo.*)

BOY.   Let me go. I want to see my mother.

KING.   My son, you shall go with me to greet your mother.

BOY.   Dushyanta is my father, not you.

KING (*smiling*).   You show I am right by contradicting me. (*Enter* ŚAKUNTALA, *wearing her hair in a single braid.*)

ŚAKUNTALA (*doubtfully*).   I have heard that All-tamer's amulet did not change when it should have done so. But I do not trust my own happiness. Yet perhaps it is as Mishrakeshi told me. (*She walks about.*)

KING (*looking at* ŚAKUNTALA. *With plaintive joy*).   It is she. It is Śakuntala.

> The pale, worn face, the careless dress,
>   The single braid,
> Show her still true, me pitiless,
>   The long vow paid.

ŚAKUNTALA (*seeing the king pale with remorse. Doubtfully*).   It is not my husband. Who is the man that soils my boy with his caresses? The amulet should protect him.

BOY (*running to his mother*).   Mother, he is a man that belongs to other people. And he calls me his son.

KING.   My darling, the cruelty I showed you has turned to happiness. Will you not recognise me?

ŚAKUNTALA (*to herself*).   Oh, my heart, believe it. Fate struck hard, but its envy is gone and pity takes its place. It is my husband.

KING.

> Black madness flies;
>   Comes memory;
> Before my eyes
>   My love I see.

> Eclipse flees far;
>   Light follows soon;
> The loving star
>   Draws to the moon.

ŚAKUNTALA.   Victory, victo—— (*Tears choke her utterance.*)

KING.

> The tears would choke you, sweet, in vain;
>   My soul with victory is fed,
> Because I see your face again—
>   No jewels, but the lips are red.

BOY.   Who is he, mother?

ŚAKUNTALA.   Ask fate, my child. (*She weeps.*)

KING.

> Dear, graceful wife, forget;
>   Let the sin vanish;
> Strangely did madness strive
>   Reason to banish.

> Thus blindness works in men,

> Love's joy to shake;
> Spurning a garland, lest
> It prove a snake.   (*He falls at her feet.*)

ŚAKUNTALA. Rise, my dear husband. Surely, it was some old sin of mine that broke my happiness—though it has turned again to happiness. Otherwise, how could you, dear, have acted so? You are so kind. (*The king rises.*) But what brought back the memory of your suffering wife?

KING. I will tell you when I have plucked out the dart of sorrow.

> 'Twas madness, sweet, that could let slip
> A tear to burden your dear lip;
> On graceful lashes seen to-day,
> I wipe it, and our grief, away.   (*He does so.*)

ŚAKUNTALA (*sees more clearly and discovers the ring*). My husband, it is the ring!

KING. Yes. And when a miracle recovered it, my memory returned.

ŚAKUNTALA. That was why it was so impossible for me to win your confidence.

KING. Then let the vine receive her flower, as earnest of her union with spring.

ŚAKUNTALA. I do not trust it. I would rather you wore it. (*Enter* MATALI.)

MATALI. I congratulate you, O King, on reunion with your wife and on seeing the face of your son.

KING. My desires bear sweeter fruit because fulfilled through a friend. Matali, was not this matter known to Indra?

MATALI (*smiling*). What is hidden from the gods? Come. Marichi's holy son, Kashyapa, wishes to see you.

KING. My dear wife, bring our son. I could not appear without you before the holy one.

ŚAKUNTALA. I am ashamed to go before such parents with my husband.

KING. It is the custom in times of festival. Come. (*They walk about.* KASHYAPA *appears seated, with* ADITI.)

KASHYAPA (*looking at the king*). Aditi,

> 'Tis King Dushyanta, he who goes before
> Your son in battle, and who rules the earth,
> Whose bow makes Indra's weapon seem no more
> Than a fine plaything, lacking sterner worth.

ADITI. His valour might be inferred from his appearance.

MATALI. O King, the parents of the gods look upon you with a glance that betrays parental fondness. Approach them.

KING. Matali,

> Sprung from the Creator's children, do I see
> Great Kashyapa and Mother Aditi?
> The pair that did produce the sun in heaven,
> To which each year twelve changing forms are given;
> That brought the king of all the gods to birth,
> Who rules in heaven, in hell, and on the earth;
> That Vishnu, than the Uncreated higher,
> Chose as his parents with a fond desire.

MATALI. It is indeed they.

KING (*falling before them*). Dushyanta, servant of Indra, does reverence to you both.

KASHYAPA. My son, rule the earth long.

ADITI. And be invincible. (ŚAKUNTALA *and her son fall at their feet.*)

KASHYAPA. My daughter,

> Your husband equals Indra, king
>   Of gods; your son is like his son;
> No further blessing need I bring:
>   Win bliss such as his wife has won.

ADITI. My child, keep the favour of your husband. And may this fine boy be an honour to the families of both parents. Come, let us be seated. (*All seat themselves.*)

KASHYAPA (*indicating one after the other*).

> Faithful Śakuntala, the boy,
>   And you, O King, I see
> A trinity to bless the world—
>   Faith, Treasure, Piety.

KING. Holy one, your favour shown to us is without parallel. You granted the fulfilment of our wishes before you called us to your presence. For, holy one,

> The flower comes first, and then the fruit;
>   The clouds appear before the rain;
> Effect comes after cause; but you
>   First helped, then made your favour plain.

MATALI. O King, such is the favour shown by the parents of the world.

KING. Holy one, I married this your maid-servant by the voluntary ceremony. When after a time her relatives brought her to me, my memory failed and I rejected her. In so doing, I sinned against Kanva, who is kin to you. But afterwards, when I saw the ring, I perceived that I had married her. And this seems very wonderful to me.

> Like one who doubts an elephant,
>   Though seeing him stride by,
> And yet believes when he has seen
>   The footprints left; so I.

KASHYAPA. My son, do not accuse yourself of sin. Your infatuation was inevitable. Listen.

KING. I am all attention.

KASHYAPA. When the nymph Menaka descended to earth and received Śakuntala, afflicted at her rejection, she came to Aditi. Then I perceived the matter by my divine insight. I saw that the unfortunate girl had been rejected by her rightful husband because of Durvasas' curse. And that the curse would end when the ring came to light.

KING (*with a sigh of relief. To himself*). Then I am free from blame.

ŚAKUNTALA (*to herself*). Thank heaven! My husband did not reject me of his own accord. He really did not remember me. I suppose I did not hear the curse in my absent-minded state, for my friends warned me most earnestly to show my husband the ring.

KASHYAPA. My daughter, you know the truth. Do not now give way to anger against your rightful husband. Remember:

> The curse it was that brought defeat and pain;
> The darkness flies; you are his queen again.
> Reflections are not seen in dusty glass,
> Which, cleaned, will mirror all the things that pass.

KING. It is most true, holy one.

KASHYAPA. My son, I hope you have greeted as he deserves the son whom Śakuntala has borne you, for whom I myself have performed the birth-rite and the other ceremonies.

KING. Holy one, the hope of my race centres in him.

KASHYAPA. Know then that his courage will make him emperor.

> Journeying over every sea,
> His car will travel easily;
> The seven islands of the earth
> Will bow before his matchless worth;
> Because wild beasts to him were tame,
> All-tamer was his common name;

As Bharata he shall be known,
For he will bear the world alone.

KING.   I anticipate everything from him, since you have performed
the rites for him.

ADITI.   Kanva also should be informed that his daughter's wishes
are fulfilled. But Menaka is waiting upon me here and cannot be
spared.

ŚAKUNTALA (*to herself*).   The holy one has expressed my own desire.

KASHYAPA.   Kanva knows the whole matter through his divine insight. (*He reflects.*) Yet he should hear from us the pleasant tidings, how
his daughter and her son have been received by her husband. Who
waits without? (*Enter a pupil.*)

PUPIL.   I am here, holy one.

KASHYAPA.   Galava, fly through the air at once, carrying pleasant
tidings from me to holy Kanva. Tell him how Durvasas' curse has come
to an end, how Dushyanta recovered his memory, and has taken
Śakuntala with her child to himself.

PUPIL.   Yes, holy one. (*Exit.*)

KASHYAPA (*to the king*).   My son, enter with child and wife the chariot of your friend Indra, and set out for your capital.

KING.   Yes, holy one.

KASHYAPA.   For now

> May Indra send abundant rain,
> Repaid by sacrificial gain;
> With aid long mutually given,
> Rule you on earth, and he in heaven.

KING.   Holy one, I will do my best.

KASHYAPA.   What more, my son, shall I do for you?

KING.   Can there be more than this? Yet may this prayer be
fulfilled.

> May kingship benefit the land,
> And wisdom grow in scholars' band;
> May Shiva see my faith on earth
> And make me free of all rebirth.

(*Exeunt omnes.*)